The Earth is Flat: Be Afraid, Be Very Afraid

They're Lying - The Earth Really is Flat

CASPER STITH

Table of Contents

Read at Your Own Risk!

Lie to Me

"History is a set of lies that people have agreed upon." - Napoleon Bonaparte

Lies permeate our lives; so prevalent that we often take them for granted.

A 2014 article on telegraph.co.uk titled *'Lies have become an accepted part of British life, poll reveals'*, provides insight into their prevalence:

The average Briton tells more than **10 lies a week**, *with two fifths claiming fibs are* **"sometimes necessary"**, *research has found.*

Almost all Britons (91%) have told a lie at some point in their lives, with a quarter (25%) saying they will "happily" tell a fib if they think it will not hurt anyone, the survey for confused.com found.

The space between *'white lies'* and outright deception is a slippery slope.

From an early age, children are taught that Santa Claus is real. We are told that Santa watches over us, determines how 'naughty or nice' we've been, and delivers gifts accordingly.

We are showered with lies before we have the capacity to think for ourselves.

Parents will often go to great lengths, and concoct elaborate stories, to maintain the *tradition.*

Passing from parents to children, the *tradition of deception* continues unabated.

The *tradition of deception*, sometimes referred to as 'the noble lie', is deeply embedded in our culture.

We eventually learn that Santa isn't real, **while much larger lies persist.**

The Big Lie

"Strange times are these in which we live when old and young are taught falsehoods in school. And the person that dares to tell the truth is called at once a lunatic and fool." - Plato

Adolf Hitler, in his 1925 book *'Mein Kampf'*, explains that when it comes to lying, it's best to go big:

*All this was inspired by the principle—which is quite true within itself—**that in the big lie there is always a certain force of credibility; because the broad masses of a nation are always more easily corrupted in the deeper strata of their emotional nature than consciously or voluntarily; and thus in the primitive simplicity of their minds they more readily fall victims to the big lie than the small lie, since they themselves often tell small lies in little matters but would be ashamed to resort to large-scale falsehoods.** It would never come into their heads to fabricate colossal untruths, and they **would not believe that others could have the impudence to distort the truth so infamously. Even though the facts which prove this to be so may be brought clearly to their minds, they will still doubt and waver and will continue to think that there may be some other explanation.** For the grossly impudent lie **always** leaves traces behind it, even after it has been nailed down, a fact which is known to all expert liars in this world and to **all who conspire together in the art of lying**.*

In 1941 Joseph Goebells, Hitler's Propaganda Minister for Nazi Germany, confirmed Hitler's message:

*The essential English leadership secret does not depend on particular intelligence. Rather, it depends on a **remarkably stupid thick-headedness**. The English follow the principle that **when one lies, one should lie big, and stick to it. They keep up their lies, even at the risk of looking ridiculous.***

The concept that the earth is a ball spinning through space is arguably the biggest lie ever told to mankind.

Not Everyone *Believes* the Earth is a Ball?

"It's easier to fool people than to convince them they've been fooled." – Mark Twain

Nikola Tesla, largely forgotten but responsible for many of the scientific breakthroughs which power our lives, describes a much different world than the one taught in schools:

Earth is a realm; it is not a planet. It is not an object; therefore, **it has no edge.** Earth would be more easily defined **as a system environment.**

Some dismiss Tesla as a crackpot, dismissing the man responsible for many of the scientific breakthroughs which power our lives. Tesla founded the alternating-current (A.C.) engine - the electrical system powering energy grids throughout the world.

Beyond A.C. electricity, Tesla is arguably the founder of radio, Wi-Fi, and radar technology, among others. Tesla had an intimate understanding of how the earth works, and was able to apply his knowledge to *real-world* projects.

Irish playwright and Nobel Prize winner George Bernard Shaw also smelled a rat:

*In the middle-ages people believed that the earth was flat, for which they had at least the evidence of their senses. We believe it to be round, not because as many as one percent of us could give physical reasons for so quaint a belief, but because **modern science has convinced us that nothing that is obvious is true, and that everything that is magical,*** *improbable, extraordinary, gigantic, microscopic, heartless, or outrageous is scientific.*

The Flat Earth Model

The concept of a flat-earth is absurd to most, but **the facts** paint a much different picture.

The concept is straightforward: The earth is not spherical, but instead a stationary plane. There are hills, valleys, mountains, oceans, and deserts, but from one to the other - **it is flat**.

The United Nations logo is essentially a flat-earth map, as viewed from directly above.

UNITED NATIONS

Divided into *33* sections, the **North Pole resides in the center** of the logo.

Antarctica is *mysteriously* absent from the logo, consistent with the flat-earth model.

Instead of Antarctica being a *mysterious* continent at the 'bottom' of the earth, the flat-earth model views Antarctica instead as an ice barrier surrounding the world's oceans.

The United Nations, on un.org, describes the original **1945** description of their logo:

*A map of the world representing an **azimuthal equidistant projection centred on the North Pole**, **inscribed in a wreath** consisting of crossed conventionalized branches of the olive tree, in gold on a field of smoke-blue with all water areas in white. The projection of the map extends to 60 degrees south latitude, and includes five concentric circles.*

Merriam-Webster.com defines '**azimuthal equidistant projection**':

*A map projection of the surface of the earth **so centered** at any given point that a straight line radiating from the center to any other point represents the shortest distance and **can be measured to scale**."*

Consistent with the globe-earth model, the *"branches of the olive tree"* in the UN logo surround the world's oceans. Traveling south from anywhere on earth will lead to Antarctica, **consistent with the globe-earth model.**

Other United Nations-related organizations, **which rely on precise measurements and distances**, also demonstrate a flat-earth.

The International Maritime Organization (IMO), the World Meteorological Organization (WMO), and the International Civil Aviation Organization (ICAO) have followed suit:

International Civil Aviation Organisation (ICAO)

A Trip 'Around' the World

While many see circumnavigation of the world as proof of a globe-earth, the same principles apply on a flat plane.

On a flat plane with the North Pole in the center, travelling in a circle always leads back to the beginning point.

*(**Title**: Gleason's new standard map of the world : on the projection of J. S. Christopher, Modern College, Blackheath, England ; scientifically and practically correct ; as "it is."; 1892)*

The flat-earth model does not imagine that earth is a flat Frisbee spinning through space, nor does it imagine an edge in which one could fall from.

Curveball

"Common sense is what tells us the earth is flat." – Albert Einstein

According to Pythagorean Geometry, the formula for earth's curvature is 8 inches multiplied by every mile, squared. For example, one mile would see 8 inches of curvature. 8 multiplied by one mile squared (one mile squared equals 1) is 8.

Two miles would see 32 inches of curvature; three miles 72 inches of curvature (6 feet); four miles would see 128 inches of curvature; 5 miles would see 200 inches of curvature, and 6 miles would see 288 inches (24 feet) of curvature; and so on.

The math should be easily testable; however no such curve can be demonstrated.

If the earth is curved by 24 feet over six miles, as the formula says it should, then surveyors, engineers, architects, and any other professions which rely on precise measurements must factor-in the curve.

Bridges, tunnels, canals, and railroads, which stretch over vast stretches of land and sea, would have to account for curvature...

But they don't.

Science Proves a Flat Earth

Oxford Dictionaries defines 'science':

the intellectual and practical activity encompassing the systematic study of the structure and behavior of the physical and natural world through **observation and experiment: "the world of science** *and technology"*

Ig Nobel Prizes take a lighter look at scientific subjects, while adhering to the scientific method.   The *silly* yet prestigious awards are described on their website, improbable.com:

The Ig Nobel Prizes honor achievements that first make people **laugh,** *and then makes them* **think.** *The prizes are intended to celebrate the unusual, honor the imaginative — and spur people's interest in science, medicine, and technology. Every year, in a gala ceremony in Harvard's Sanders Theatre, 1200 splendidly eccentric spectators watch the winners step forward to accept their Prizes. These are physically handed out by genuinely bemused genuine Nobel laureates.*

In 2003, the contest featured an obscure experiment, in which scientists set out to prove that the U.S. state Kansas is as *"flat as a pancake."*

A September, 2003, The Guardian published an article titled, '**Is Kansas flat as a pancake?** *No,* **it's flatter,** *say the scientists who actually bothered to find out.'*

The comparison is silly, but the conclusion is one that shatters the ball-earth myth. The article describes the findings:

This year, for instance, three geographers compared the flatness of Kansas to the flatness of a pancake. They used **topographic data** *from a digital scale model* **prepared by the US Geological Survey,** *and they*

12

purchased a pancake from the International House of Pancakes. If perfect flatness were a value of 1.00, they reported, the calculated flatness of a pancake would be 0.957 "which is pretty flat, but far from perfectly flat". **Kansas's flatness however turned out to be 0.997**, *which they said might be described,* **mathematically,** *as "damn flat".*

The conclusion that Kansas is almost perfectly flat could be seen as an anomaly, however all U.S. states were subsequently tested.

In 2014, the American Geographical Society published an article titled, *'The flatness of U. S. states'.*

The article demonstrates that flatness is not the exception, **but the rule:**

A new study measured the flatness of U. S. states and found that (a) Florida is by far the flattest state, (b) Kansas is not as flat as most people think, and (c) **all states are flatter than a pancake**.

A September, 2014, article on mentalfloss.com titled, *'Is Kansas Really Flatter than a Pancake?'*, is one of the few mainstream publications to hint at the explosive nature of the result:

When the playful study first came out in the Annals of Improbable Research, Lee Allison, then the Director of the Kansas Geological Survey, quipped that **"everything on Earth is flatter than the pancake as they measured it."**

Clarifying Allison's retort in a paper from earlier this year, geographers Jerome Dobson and Joshua Campbell explain it like this:

"The pancake measured in the article was 130 millimeters, and its surface relief was 2 millimeters. Apply that ratio to the east-west dimension of Kansas, approximately 644 kilometers, and the state would need a mountain (2/130 x 664,000 meters) 9,908 meters tall in order not to be flatter than a pancake. Since the highest mountain in the world is 8,848 meters tall, **every state in the U.S. is flatter than a pancake."**

13

Since pancakes and flat objects don't curve, arc, or bend, the conclusion that all U.S. states are flatter than a pancake is amusing on the surface, but **the implications are astounding**.

The distance from Los Angeles to New York is around 2,500 miles, which - according to earthcurvature.com — means that there should be **763 miles of earth curvature in the span**, which is impossible if all U.S. states are *"flatter than a pancake."*

There are plenty of mainstream articles surrounding the studies, **but not one** highlighting the explosive implications.

Anomalies

The first *'actual'* image from space occurred in 1972, around the time of the fifth 'manned mission' to the moon.

The image portrays the earth as a **perfectly spherical** body:

(1972; image courtesy of NASA)

All official images of the earth show a perfectly circular globe, but the scientific establishment **now** indicates that the earth is actually *"**pear-shaped**."*

Astrophysicist Neal DeGrasse Tyson is considered by many to be *the* expert when it comes to physics, planets and space.

(2014 image of Bill Nye 'the science guy', Barack Obama, and Neil DeGrasse Tyson)

Famousscientists.org describes the *importance* of Tyson:

One of today's popularizers of science, *Neil deGrasse Tyson is a science communicator and known American astrophysicist. Currently, he is the Hayden Planetarium's Frederick P. Rose director at the Rose Center for Earth and Space. He is also one of the research associates of the American Museum of Natural History's department of astrophysics. Since he is a **popularizer of science**, he has appeared in television shows such as NOVA ScienceNow which was aired on PBS from 2006-2011. He is involved in fields such as physical cosmology, astrophysics, and* **science communication.**

Tyson is also well-connected within governmental and political circles (the article continues):

Former US President **George W. Bush had appointed Neil deGrasse Tyson to be a member of the Commission on the Future of the United States Aerospace Industry**. *Two years later, he served as a part of the* **President's Commission on Implementation of United States Space Exploration Policy**. *This Commission is better known by its more popular nickname which is the "Moon, Mars, and Beyond" commission. After a short while, he was then* **awarded by NASA their Distinguished Public Service Medal which happens to be the highest honor NASA awards to civilians.**

All 'official' pictures of the earth show a perfect sphere, but Tyson <u>explains</u> how looks can be deceiving:

*Sea level at the equator is farther away from the center of the earth than sea level near the poles. When you spin pizza dough, it **kind of flattens out**.*

So earth, throughout its life, when it formed it was spinning, and it got a little wider at the equator than it does at the poles.

It's not actually a sphere... it's oblate. Officially it's an oblate-spheroid; that's what we call it.

*But not only that, it's slightly wider below the equator than above the equator; **a little chubbier**. **It's like pear-shaped**. It turns out the pear-shapedness is bigger than the height of Mt. Everest above sea-level.*

Planes

There are many aspects of air travel which defy logic, but we take them for granted because that's what we've been taught.

Airplanes should logically have to lower their trajectory periodically to avoid moving further and further away from the earth. An airplane traveling 500 miles per hour on a globe would have to dip their nose about a mile every five minutes to avoid flying off into the atmosphere, but no such corrections occur.

We are told that gravity keeps everything at a constant, so essentially everything within the earth's atmosphere is spinning eastward – in unison and undetectable to those within it - at **over 1000 miles per hour**. If that was the case, a plane flying westward – going against the eastward spin - should face a headwind of 1000 miles per hour – but that is also not the case.

While going against the spin of the earth isn't a factor for airplanes' flight times and gas mileage, space agencies apparently use it to their advantage. A 2016 article on space.com titled '*How Fast Is Earth Moving?*' describes the *interesting* phenomenon:

Space agencies love to take advantage of Earth's spin. *If they're sending humans to the International Space Station, for example, the preferred location to do so is close to the equator. That's why space* *shuttle missions used to launch from Florida.* **By doing so and launching in the same direction as Earth's spin, rockets get a speed boost to help them fly into space.**

When looking out from a plane or hot-air balloon, **the horizon is always flat**.

Merriam-webster.com defines horizon as follows:

the line where the earth seems to meet the sky : the apparent junction of earth and sky

As we ascend and reach peak height, **the horizon always remains consistent with the observer's eye level,** which is what *should* occur on a flat-plane.

Digital simulations which compare ascension from a round object versus ascension from a flat-plane clearly demonstrate that we reside on a flat-plane. When ascending from a spherical object, spinning or otherwise, the horizon recedes, forcing the observer to continually adjust their gaze downward to view the horizon.

The distance to the horizon is not impacted by 'curvature of the earth', it is instead determined by the strength of the lens and the density of elements in the air, such as gases, moisture, and heat.

A zoom lens or telescope **always** extends the horizon beyond what the naked eye can see.

When looking up, it seems as though we can see forever. Air density decreases with altitude, allowing us to see much further upward than outward.

An article on usatoday.com titled *'Understanding air pressure'* describes the phenomena:

How pressure decreases with altitude

As you go higher in the air, the atmospheric pressure decreases.

The exact pressure at a particular altitude depends of weather conditions, but a couple of approximations and a formula can give you a general idea of how pressure decreases with altitude.

A rule of thumb for the altimeter correction is that the pressure drops about 1 inch of mercury for each 1,000 foot altitude gain. If you're using millibars, the correction is 1 millibar for each 8 meters of altitude gain. These rules work quite well for elevations or altitudes of less than two or three thousand feet.

The standard atmosphere is a table giving values of air pressure, temperature and air density for various altitudes from the ground up. You can think of these values as averages for the entire Earth over the course of a year.

Where's the Curve?

Space agencies and those in the 'space' business claim that somewhere 'up there' the earth stops looking flat and starts looking spherical.

There is no definitive information regarding the altitude which the earth supposedly begins to show its curvature. We are told that the change simply occurs somewhere along the way to space, and the only *evidence* are 'photos', 'videos', and 'first-hand' accounts.

There is no footage demonstrating a point in which the earth stops looking flat and begins appearing spherical.

Trains

Railroads are integral to commerce and industry, so ensuring that the tracks remains level is paramount.

Railroads cover vast swaths of land, and minor mistakes in their construction have tremendous consequences.

If train tracks are being laid over an *"oblate-spheroid,"* then the tracks **must** gradually curve by varying degrees - **but they don't.**

There are highly complex formulas used to ensure that trains make precise turns, but none to account for the *'natural curvature of the earth'.*

Railroad tracks are perfectly flat for thousands of miles, which is impossible on a curved surface.

South African author Thomas Winship, author of the 1899 book titled, *'Zetetic Cosmogony; or Conclusive Evidence that the World is not a Rotating Revolving Globe but a Stationary Plane Circle'*, describes his findings:

J.C. Bourne in his book, "The History of the Great Western Railway" stated that the entire original English railroad, more than 118 miles long, that the whole line with the exception of the inclined planes, may be regarded practically as level. The British Parliament Session in 1862 that approved its construction recorded in Order No. 44 for the proposed railway, "That the section be drawn to the same HORIZONTAL scale as the plan, and to a vertical scale of not less than one inch to every one hundred feet, and shall show the surface of the ground marked on the plan, the intended level of the proposed work, the height of every embankment, and the depth of every cutting, **and a DATUM HORIZONTAL LINE which shall be the same throughout the whole length of the work.***"*

One hundred and eighteen miles of level railway, **and yet the surface on which it is projected a globe? Impossible. It cannot be.** *Early in 1898 I met Mr. Hughes, chief officer of the steamer 'City of Lincoln.' This gentleman told me he had projected thousands of miles of level railway in South America,* **and never heard of any allowance for curvature being made.** *On one occasion he surveyed* <u>over one thousand miles of railway which was a perfect straight line all the way.</u> **It is well known that in the Argentine Republic and other parts of South America, there are railways thousands of miles long without curve or gradient. In projecting railways, the world is acknowledged to be a plane, and if it were a globe the rules of projection have yet to be discovered. Level railways prove a level world, to the utter confusion of the globular school of impractical men with high salaries and little brains.**

The Trans-Siberian Railway runs over 5,700 miles (over 9,100 kilometers), making countless horizontal turns throughout.

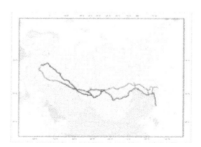

Construction of such a massive project – if also having to account for earth's *"pear-shaped"* curvature - would be next to impossible.

The world's longest bridge is the Danyang–Kunshan Grand Bridge in China, which is a viaduct for the Beijing–Shanghai High-Speed Railway. At over 102 miles (164 kilometers), the viaduct is a modern engineering miracle, employing 10,000 people and costing over $8.5 billion.

Surprisingly, there is no mention of how the impossible task of curving the bridge over a *"pear-shaped"* surface was accomplished.

Automobiles

In the steel construction industry, *"curvature"* relates to horizontal curves, and nothing to do with the 'natural curvature of the earth'.

The *'Plan curvature in bridges'* is described on steelconstruction.info:

*Although very many bridges **follow a straight alignment from one abutment to the other**, some are partly or wholly **curved** in plan. For road bridges, **curvature may be required to optimise the layout of the carriageway**. For footbridges, curvature may be employed **either for a more interesting aspect for users or to enhance the appearance**. Railway bridges are rarely curved in plan, since the track radius is normally so great that the deviation from straight over a span is modest and easily accommodated on a straight superstructure.*

An example of the *"curvature"* is shown below:

The Lake Pontchartrain Causeway holds the distinction for being the longest bridge over water in the world.

("satellite" photo of the Lake Pontchartrain Causeway)

Just shy of 24 miles (38 kilometers), any mention of how the construction could possibly have occurred over the *"pear-shaped"* world is also *mysteriously* absent.

If the earth's curvature was not factored into the longest bridges in the world, it obviously was not factored into the shorter ones.

The 'curvature of the earth' is not factored into any projects because it does not exist.

Water – Nature's Level

*"There are rivers that flow for hundreds of miles towards the level of the sea without falling more than a few feet — notably, **the Nile, which, in a thousand miles, falls but a foot.** A level expanse of this extent is quite incompatible with the idea of the Earth's convexity. It is, therefore, a reasonable proof that Earth is not a globe."* – Samuel Rowbotham; *'A hundred proofs the Earth is not a Globe'; **1885***

Covering roughly seventy-five percent of the earth's surface, **water always seeks its own level.**

If we were living on a curved surface, one of water's properties would be its curvature; however that is not the case.

In fact, water is the most precise level possible. It is also worth noting that 'level' means **perfectly flat**, and not curved over long distances.

Water levels are so precise that they can be relied on for professional construction projects.

Professional Deck Builder magazine, at Deckmagazine.com, describes the precision of water-levels in an article titled *'Making and Using a Water Level'*:

*For about the same cost as putting a half tank of gas in a small pickup, you can build a leveling device that is **as accurate** and versatile as the most expensive rotating laser level or optical transit on the market. In fact, this low-cost level can do a few tricks that neither of those top-of-the-line tools can do at any price — "seeing through" or leveling around obstructions, for instance.*

The article continues:

*...an ancient tool that works on the principle that **water always seeks its own level**. Fill a long, flexible tube with liquid, and the liquid at both ends will be at the same level whether you're holding them together **or spreading them a hundred feet apart.***

Water seeks its own level by flowing downhill. This fact is arguably common sense, though it is often attributed to gravity. The United States Geological Survey, on its website usgs.gov, describes the phenomenon:

*One word can explain why any river exists on Earth—gravity. You've heard that "water seeks its own level," but really water is seeking the center of the Earth, just like everything else. In practical terms, water generally seeks to flow to the oceans, which are at sea level. So, **no matter where on Earth water is, it tries to flow downhill**. With the Earth being a very unlevel place, water ends up occupying the valleys and depressions in the landscape as rivers and lakes.*

The myth that water flows down the drain in a different direction depending on the hemisphere, referred to as **Coriolis force** (also referred to as *'fictitious force'*), is not based on facts. The Library of Congress verifies that the actual explanation which determines how water goes down a drain is much less complicated:

*It all depends upon **how the water was introduced and the geometric structure of the drain**.*

The properties of water are simple and straightforward, and not consistent with how liquid on an *"oblate-spheroid"* would behave.

Ships in the Distance

*"We assume the convexity of water, because we have **no other way to explain the appearance and disappearance of ships at sea**."* – Thomas Huxley (Charles Darwin's grandfather)

Many people assume the earth is flat because ships disappear at sea as they get further way, but this myth is easily disproven.

Using a zoom lens, one can see objects which are no longer visible to the naked eye. Boats and distant land masses can be seen *many* miles beyond where they are *supposed* to, proving that the 'official' earth curvature formula is not accurate.

If we were living on a curved surface, objects in the distance would begin leaning, or tilting backward, but instead objects in the distance remain perfectly vertical, as demonstrated below.

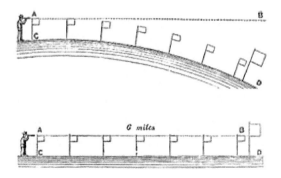

(images from Samuel Rowbotham's 'Zetetic Astronomy: Earth Not a Globe')

Spin Doctors

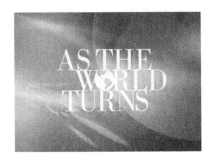

The earth is said to be spinning at a rate of over **1,000 miles per hour** on an invisible axis. The earth is said to be rotating around the sun at over **67,000 miles per hour**, causing us to whip through the Milky Way galaxy at over **500,000 miles per hour**.

All the while, the Milky Way galaxy is purportedly expanding at the speed of light, traveling roughly **670 million miles per hour.**

With the earth purportedly traversing over **21 million miles per day**, one would expect vertigo and dizziness to be a way of life, but that is not the case.

Webmd.com describes the causes of motion sickness:

*You get motion sickness when one part of your balance-sensing system (your inner ear , eyes, and sensory nerves) senses that your body is moving, but the other parts don't. For example, if you are in the cabin of a moving ship, your inner ear may sense the motion of waves, but your eyes don't see any movement. **This conflict between the senses** causes motion sickness.*

We experience motion sickness from trains, from planes, in cars, on elevators; in all situations where motion is involved, **but not from the motion of the rapidly-spinning earth.**

In a Cornell University article titled *'Can we feel the Earth spin?'* explains why we are *oblivious* to the incessant spin of the earth:

At the equator, the Earth is spinning at 1000 miles per hour about its axis and moving at 67,000 miles per hour around the Sun. With all this motion, you would expect to feel something, right? **Well we don't feel anything because all of the motions are almost completely constant.**

When you take a really smooth plane or train ride, you don't feel the motion unless the plane/train slows down, speeds up, or hits a bump in the road. *So as long as there is constant motion, we don't feel it.*

The article goes on to compare the earth's spin to an *"amusement park ride"*:

Above we said that the Earth spinning is an example of almost constant motion. The reason we said "almost" is that the Earth's spin carries us around in a circle, not in a straight line. It's a very big circle, and it takes a long time to go around, but qualitatively it is the **same thing that happens on a spinning amusement park ride, where it feels like you're being flung outward as the ride spins around.**

We accept these conclusions because that is what we've been taught, but they defy our common sense and logic.

When riding a merry-go-round, the spin is apparent. If we imagine an ant on a large merry-go-round, or a human on an extremely large merry-go-round, it would **always be obvious to the subject** that they are in-motion.

The current model of a spinning-ball earth has no basis in reality.

Don't Mind the Wobble

Not only is the earth supposedly spinning at over 1,000 miles per hour, we're also told that it's **wobbling.**

In an April, 2016 nasa.gov article titled *'NASA Study Solves Two Mysteries About Wobbling Earth',* NASA explains the wobble:

*Earth does not always spin on an axis running through its poles. Instead, it **wobbles irregularly over time**, drifting toward North America throughout most of the 20th Century. That direction has **changed drastically** due to changes in water mass on Earth.*

NASA describes how the *"irregular"* wobble has *"changed drastically,"* but still not enough for one person on earth to be able to notice it.

The article continues to explain a recent *"abrupt turn"* of the *"spin axis"*:

*Around the year 2000, Earth's spin axis took an **abrupt turn toward the east and is now drifting almost twice as fast as before,** at a rate of almost 7 inches (17 centimeters) a year. "It's no longer moving toward Hudson Bay, but instead toward the British Isles," said Adhikari. "**That's a massive swing.**" Adhikari and Ivins set out to explain this unexpected change.*

The Pole Star

*"I am **constant as the northern star,***
Of whose true-fix'd and resting quality
*There is no fellow in the **firmament.**"*

-Julius Caesar; by Shakespeare

Polaris, also known as the North Star, resides directly above the North Pole.

'Science' places Polaris at approximately 323 light-years from the sun, revised *slightly* lower from the prior 434 light-year figure.

Polaris was and is still used as a valuable navigational tool due to its fixed nature in the sky.

(45 minute exposure of Polaris and nearby stars making perfect circular orbits)

'Stars' and 'planets' make perfect circular rotations around Polaris, which would not be possible if earth was an *"oblate-spheroid"* hurtling chaotically through a rapidly expanding universe.

If the earth was indeed an *"oblate-spheroid"* spinning on its axis, then the South Pole would have similar attributes to those of the North Pole, but it doesn't.

One oneminuteastronomer.com, an article titled 'How to Find the South Celestial Pole' describes why "bad luck" is to blame for the massive discrepancy between the North and 'South Pole':

In the northern hemisphere, the bright and easy-to-find star Polaris marks the position of the north celestial pole. This makes it **easy for stargazers and navigators to find north,** and get oriented in the night sky.

But in the southern hemisphere, it is different.

By sheer bad luck, the south celestial pole (SCP), the imaginary point in the sky directly above the Earth's South Pole, coincides with no bright star, and the southern polar sky has few other guides to find the pole.

Evidence

- *1. the available body of facts or information indicating whether a belief or proposition is true or valid: (Oxford Dictionaries)*

While most *believe* the earth to be spherical, there is *no tangible physical evidence* proving the case.

If the earth is indeed spherical, a sixth-grade class project should be able to easily demonstrate it as such, **but that's not the case.**

There are no physical tests that can be performed to demonstrate that the earth is spherical. To the contrary, all physical tests definitively point to a flat-earth.

With no firsthand or tangible evidence of earth's curvature, we rely on videos and images passed on to the public from 'official' sources.

Circumstantial Evidence – **(thefreedictionary.com)** *- Information and testimony presented by a party in a civil or* **criminal action** *that* **permit conclusions that indirectly establish the existence or nonexistence of a fact or event** *that the party seeks to prove.*

Trust Us, We're NASA

"NASA's vision: We reach for new heights and reveal the unknown for the benefit of humankind." – nasa.gov

Almost all of the evidence 'proving' the earth to be an *"oblate-spheroid"* comes from one place, therefore a closer look into the source is warranted.

The following is a brief history of NASA, as described by NASA (on nasa.gov):

President Dwight D. Eisenhower established the National Aeronautics and Space Administration in 1958, partially in response to the Soviet Union's launch of the first artificial satellite the previous year. NASA grew out of the National Advisory Committee on Aeronautics (NACA), which had been researching flight technology for more than 40 years.

President John F. Kennedy focused NASA and the nation on sending astronauts to the moon by the end of the 1960s. Through the Mercury and Gemini projects, NASA developed the technology and skills it needed for the journey. On July 20, 1969, Neil Armstrong and Buzz Aldrin became the first of 12 men to walk on the moon, meeting Kennedy's challenge.

Meanwhile, NASA was continuing the aeronautics research pioneered by NACA. It also conducted purely scientific research and worked on developing applications for space technology, combining both pursuits in developing the first weather and communications satellites.

After Apollo, NASA focused on creating a reusable ship to provide regular access to space: the space shuttle. First launched in 1981, the space shuttle flew more than 130 successful missions before being retired in 2011. In 2000, the United States and Russia established permanent human presence in space aboard the International Space Station, a multinational project representing the work of 15 nations.

NASA also has continued its scientific research. In 1997, Mars Pathfinder became the first in a fleet of spacecraft that have been exploring Mars, as we try to determine whether life ever existed there. The Terra, Aqua and Aura Earth Observing System satellites are flagships of a different fleet, this one in Earth orbit, designed to help us understand how our home world is changing. NASA's aeronautics teams are focused on improving aviation, so it meets the explosive growth in global demand for air services.

Throughout its history, NASA has conducted or funded research that has led to numerous improvements to life here on Earth.

Most believe that NASA was established to benefit humanity, but a deeper look paints a much more complex – and troubling - picture.

NASA has Secrets?

The general public trusts NASA, and it is largely assumed that its sole purpose was for mankind's betterment.

A closer look reveals an organization that more closely resembles an intelligence agency.

Recently declassified documents show that the agency is deeply entrenched in the intelligence world, involved in numerous **black-ops** (defined by dictionary.com: *a secret mission or campaign carried out by a military, governmental, or other organization, typically one in which the organization **conceals or denies its involvement***).

An April 10, 2015, article titled *'NASA's Secret Relationships with U.S. Defense and Intelligence Agencies'* explores these connections.

Published at *'The National Security Archive'* at The George Washington University (nsarchive.gwu.edu), the introduction to the report exposes the secrecy:

Furnishing cover stories for covert operations, *monitoring Soviet missile tests, and supplying weather data to the U.S. military have been part of the secret side of the National Aeronautics and Space Administration (NASA) since its inception in 1958, according to declassified documents posted for the first time today by the National Security Archive at The George Washington University (www.nsarchive.org).*

James E. David, a curator in NASA's Division of Space History, obtained the documents in the course of researching his critically praised book, Spies and Shuttles: NASA's Secret Relationships with the DoD and CIA (University Press of Florida, 2015). David has compiled, edited and introduced more than 50 of these records for today's posting.

Even though Congress's intention in forming NASA was to establish a purely civilian space agency, according to David a **combination of circumstances led the agency to commingle its activities with black programs operated by the U.S. military and Intelligence Community.**

In order to understand how NASA became tangled up in covert operations, it is important to understand its history.

The Backdrop

Beginning in 1945, the US government launched 'Operation Paperclip'. The 'Operation' brought over 1,500 Nazi-German scientists to the United States in order to continue their *projects* and *research.*

A 2006 report, published by the US Justice Department and spanning 600 pages, was reviewed in-depth by the New York Times.

In a 2010 article titled *'Nazis Were Given 'Safe Haven' in U.S., Report Says'*, the New York Times exposes the hypocrisy of the 'Operation':

*Perhaps the report's most damning disclosures come in assessing the Central Intelligence Agency's involvement with Nazi émigrés. Scholars and previous government reports had acknowledged the C.I.A.'s use of Nazis for postwar intelligence purposes. But this report goes further in documenting the level of American **complicity and deception** in such operations.*

*The Justice Department report, describing what it calls "the government's **collaboration with persecutors**," says that O.S.I investigators learned that some of the Nazis "were indeed knowingly granted entry" to the United States, even though government officials were aware of their pasts. "America, which prided itself on being a safe haven for the persecuted, became — in some small measure — a **safe haven for persecutors** as well," it said.*

Not surprisingly, many of these *Nazi émigrés* ended up in key positions.

Declassified documents also show that not all of these *émigrés* were noble, or even documented for that matter. In summarizing *'Foreign Scientist Case Files 1945-1958'*, archives.gov provides an overview of the documents from that timeframe:

*This series consists of personnel dossiers on over 1,500 German and other foreign scientists, technicians, and engineers who were brought to the United States under Project Paperclip and similar programs. Among the dossiers are those on Georg Rickhey, a former official at the Nordhausen underground V-2 rocket factory who arrived in 1946 but who left the United States in 1947 when he was tried (and acquitted) for war crimes by a U.S. military tribunal; Walter Schreiber, who had been instrumental in medical experiments on concentration camp inmates and who fled the United States to Argentina in 1952 after the appearance of a newspaper column about his activities; and, Arthur Rudolph who had been a V-2 project engineer and who left the United States in 1984 following the Department of Justice's discovery of his role in the persecution of prisoners at the Nordhausen factory. **Not included among the dossiers is one for rocket scientist Wernher von Braun. It was never transferred to NARA**.*

The Man, The Myth, The Nazi

Wernher von Braun, one of the most important NASA scientists in its history, was a former member of the Nazi Party, as well as a member of the highly-controversial 'SS'.

In a 2014 article in businessinsider.com titled '*9 Nazi Scientists Who Helped Build The American Space Program*' profiles Von Braun, demonstrating his importance to 'the program'.

A 2001 description of Von Braun, published on nasa.gov, describes his importance to the '*space program*', while avoiding any direct mention of his Nazi or SS past:

Wernher von Braun is, **without doubt, the greatest rocket scientist in history.** *His crowning achievement, as head of NASA's Marshall Space Flight Center, was to* **lead the development of the Saturn V booster rocket that helped land the first men on the Moon in July 1969.**

It is important to note that Von Braun first gained prominence for creating high-powered weaponry, which was used against densely populated urban areas, notably London - which was a U.S. ally during World War II (the article continues):

*He designed the V-2 rocket that was **used so effectively against Britain** during World War II.*

Von Braun claims that his involvement with the Nazi s and SS was more out of necessity than intent; if he wanted to keep his lifelong dream of 'space travel' alive, he had no choice but to join 'the party', he claimed.

Let's Go to the Moon!

With the U.S. caught-up in the Cold War with the Soviet Union, the *'race to space'* became a focal point in international affairs.

In a 1961 address to Congress, U.S. President John F. Kennedy made a bold assertion:

*I believe that this nation should commit itself to achieving the goal, **before this decade is out, of landing a man on the moon and returning him safely to the earth.** No single space project in this period will be more impressive to mankind, or more important for the long-range exploration of space.*

Von Braun and his team were being put to the test. Based on Von Braun's prior research, this task was impossible.

In 1953, Von Braun published a book titled *'Conquest of the Moon'*. In the book, Von Braun explains the difficulties with travelling to the moon and back:

*It is commonly believed that man will fly directly from the earth to the moon, but to do this, we would **require a vehicle of such gigantic proportions that it would prove an economic impossibility.***

*Calculations have been carefully worked out on the type of vehicle we would need for the non-stop flight from the earth to the moon, and to return. The figures speak for themselves. **Three rockets would be necessary.***

*It would have to develop sufficient speed to penetrate the atmosphere and overcome the earth's gravity and, having traveled all the way to the moon, **it must still have enough fuel to land safely and make the return trip to earth.***

*Furthermore, in order to give the expedition a margin of safety, we would not use one ship alone, but a **minimum of three ... each rocket ship would be taller than New York's Empire State Building** and weigh about **ten times the tonnage of the Queen Mary, or some 800,000 tons**.*

Despite the obstacles, in 1969 the U.S. claimed to have successfully flown men to the moon and back.

It is important to note that there were no major 'space travel' breakthroughs between Von Braun's 1953 claims and the 1969 flight to the moon and back.

The Saturn V rocket, which was used to purportedly travel to the moon and back, weighed 2,950 tons, much less than the 800,000 tons Von Braun estimated in 1953.

A 2014 article on space.com titled *'Apollo 11's Vintage Tech: The Most Amazing Moon Landing Innovations'* explains how NASA was able to do so much, with so little:

*While the Apollo 11 landing was on the **cutting-edge of technology in 1969**, today it's a demonstration of how much could be accomplished **with so little**.*

The computing technology of the average cell phone far exceeds the combined computing power of the two spacecraft that got humans to the moon and home safely.

From 1969 through 1972, NASA claims to have sent six manned missions to the moon. Surprisingly, **we haven't been back since.**

The Van Allen Belts

The Van Allen radiation belts surround the earth. The belts begin at around 400 miles above earth, and extend to a purported 36,000 miles outward.

In a 2014 article published on nasa.gov titled *'NASA's Van Allen Probes Spot an Impenetrable Barrier in Space'*, describes the biggest hurdle for space travel:

*Two donuts of **seething radiation** that surround Earth, called the Van Allen radiation belts, have been found to contain a nearly **impenetrable barrier** that prevents the fastest, most energetic electrons from reaching Earth.*

Powerful electrons are unable to breach the belts, but brave men with 1969 technology were able to seamlessly power their way through.

James Van Allen, credited with discovering the Van Allen belt, was aware that the radiation within the belts prevented space travel. In a 1959 article in Scientific American, Van Allen describes the belts:

*Our **measurements** show that the maximum radiation level as of 1958 is equivalent to between **10 and 100 roentgens per hour**, depending on the still-undetermined proportion of protons to electrons. Since a human being **exposed for two days to even 10 roentgens would have only an even chance of survival**, the **radiation belts obviously present an obstacle to space flight.***

A 2012 article on Smithsonian.com titled *'Going Nuclear Over the Pacific'* explains how the Van Allen Belts crushed any dreams of space travel:

46

Knowledge of radiation in space was still fragmentary and new. It was only four years before that James A. Van Allen, a University of Iowa physicist who had been experimenting with Geiger counters on satellites, claimed to have discovered that the planet was encircled by a **"deadly band of X-rays,"** and that radiation from the sun **"hit the satellites so rapidly and furiously"** that the devices jammed. Van Allen announced his findings on May 1, 1958, at a joint meeting of the National Academy of Sciences and the American Physical Society, and the following day, the Chicago Tribune *bannered the headline,* **"Radiation Belt Dims Hope of Space Travel."** *The story continued:* **"Death, lurking in a belt of unexpectedly heavy radiation about 700 miles above the earth, today dimmed man's dreamed of conquering outer space."**

News of the **"hot band of peril"** *immediately cast doubt on whether Laika, the Russian dog, would have been able to survive for a week in space aboard Sputnik II, as the Soviets claimed, in November of 1957. (The Soviets said that after six days, the dog's oxygen ran out and she was euthanized with poisoned food. It was later learned that Laika, the first live animal to be launched into space,* **died just hours after the launch from overheating** *and stress, when a* **malfunction in the capsule caused the temperature to rise.)**

What Van Allen had discovered were the **bands of high-energy particles that were held in place by strong magnetic fields,** *and soon known as the Van Allen Belts. A year later, he appeared on the cover of* Time *magazine as he* **opened an <u>entirely new field of research</u>**— *magnetospheric physics—and* **<u>catapulted the United States into the race</u>** *to space with the Soviet Union.*

On the same day Van Allen held his press conference in May 1958, he agreed to cooperate with the U.S. military on a top-secret project. The plan: **to send atomic bombs into space in an attempt to blow up the Van Allen Belts**, or to at least disrupt them with a massive blast of nuclear energy.

A 2010 article on NPR.org, titled 'A Very Scary Light Show: Exploding H-Bombs In Space', describes the ingenious plan to blast through the belts:

Discover It, Then Blow It Up

The plan was to send rockets hundreds of miles up, higher than the Earth's atmosphere, and then detonate nuclear weapons to see: a) If a bomb's radiation would make it harder to see what was up there (like incoming Russian missiles!); b) If an explosion would do any damage to objects nearby; c) If the Van Allen belts would move a blast down the bands to an earthly target (Moscow! for example); and — **most peculiar — d) if a man-made explosion might "alter" the natural shape of the belts.**

The scientific basis for these proposals **is not clear**. Fleming is trying to figure out if Van Allen had any theoretical reason to suppose the military could use the Van Allen belts to attack a hostile nation. He supposes that at the height of the Cold War, the most pressing argument for a military experiment was, "if we don't do it, the Russians will." And, indeed, the Russians did test atomic bombs and hydrogen bombs in space.

In any case, says the science history professor, **"this is the first occasion I've ever discovered where someone discovered something and immediately decided to blow it up."**

One could almost believe that the military was trying to blast a hole through a physical barrier, but according to modern 'science', the concept is absurd.

Detonating high-powered weaponry high above earth was not without consequences. A 2014 Popular Science article titled 'Apollo Rocketed Through the Van Allen Belts' describes the fallout of the 'experiment', which was actually just done to test how the earth would do *in a nuclear war*:

NASA never tried to clear the Van Allen belt with a nuclear bomb, but an Atomic Energy Commission test in 1962 briefly **made the radiation problem much worse.**

America's nuclear testing program of the early 1960s was called

*Operation Dominic. Within this program was a group of atmospheric tests called the **Fishbowl** events designed to understand how nuclear weapon debris would interact with the Earth's magnetic field in the event of nuclear war. The highest of the **Fishbowl** events was one called **Starfish Prime** (the first attempt, Starfish, had failed). **This test saw a 1.4 megaton bomb detonate at an <u>altitude of 250 miles</u>. Rather than clear out the inner Van Allen belt, Starfish Prime added more radiation around the planet.***

The Orion 'spacecraft' is currently (early 2017) being built by NASA *"to take humans farther than they've ever gone before. Orion will serve as the exploration vehicle that will carry the crew to space, provide emergency abort capability, sustain the crew during the space travel, and provide safe re-entry from deep space return velocities."*

In 2012, NASA engineer Kelly Smith explains the obstacles faced by Orion:

As we get further away from earth we'll pass through the van Allen belts, an area of dangerous radiation. **Radiation like this could harm the guidance system on board computers, or other electronics on Orion. Naturally we have to pass through this danger zone twice.** *Once up and once back.*

But Orion has protection. Shielding will be put to the test as the vehicle cuts through the waves of radiation. Sensors aboard will record radiation levels for scientists to study. **We must solve these challenges before we send people through these regions of space.**

In a 2014 article on huffingtonpost.co.uk titled '*NASA 'Admitted To Apollo Hoax' In Orion Video, Say Obviously Mistaken Conspiracy Theorists*', we are informed that the astronauts weren't in the Van Allen belt long enough to be impacted by the deadly radiation:

*The answer, simply, and which has been explained in detail elsewhere, is that the Apollo astronauts **were not in the Van Allen belt for long enough to have to deal with dangerous levels of exposure to radiation**.*

*The Apollo astronauts did return to Earth having been exposed to **significant radiation - but not more than is allowed by US law for workers at nuclear power stations**, for instance.*

This certainly defies the earlier assessment (Scientific American article in 1959) made by Dr. James Van Allen, which was based on *actual* Geiger counter data obtained from an unmanned probe launched towards the belts.

It Gets 'Wild'

In a 2002 documentary titled *'Astronauts Gone Wild'*, (available on youtube.com), researcher Bart Sibrel interviews Apollo astronauts about their purported trips to the moon.

At the 13:40 mark of the movie, Sibrel questions Alan Beam, astronaut on Apollo 12 (1969), about his experience with the *deadly* Van Allen radiation belt:

Sibrel: "Any ill effects from the Van Allen Radiation belts?"

Beam: **"I am not sure we went far enough out to encounter the Van Allen radiation belts. Maybe we did."**

Sibrel then explains to Beam that the belts begin at around 1,000 miles out and extent to around 25,000 miles out.

Beam: **"Then we went right out through them."**

Sibrel: "No effects on yourselves?"

Beam: "Uh-uh, **didn't even know it. I don't think anyone even, well, maybe someone said 'you went through the radiation belt', but we didn't feel it inside. And we didn't get any added radiation.***"*

Predictably, the Geiger counter readings from the Apollo missions are considered 'classified' and unavailable to the public.

In 2013, NASA discovered new information surrounding the Van Allen belts. In a nasa.gov article titled *'NASA's Van Allen Probes Reveal a New Radiation Belt Around Earth'*, NASA explains how, despite six 'manned missions to the moon', they have *now* discovered a third radiation belt:

NASA's Van Allen Probes mission has discovered a **previously unknown** third radiation belt around Earth, revealing the existence of unexpected structures and processes within these hazardous regions of space.

Previous observations of Earth's Van Allen belts have long documented two distinct regions of trapped radiation surrounding our planet. Particle detection instruments aboard the twin Van Allen Probes, launched Aug. 30, quickly revealed to scientists the existence of this new, transient, third radiation belt.

A Funny Thing Happened...

*"There are great ideas undiscovered; breakthroughs available to those who can remove **truth's protective layers.**"* - Neil Armstrong; 'first man to set foot on the moon'; 1994; speaking at the White House commemoration of the 25th anniversary of the Apollo 11 mission

Bart Sibrel's *'Astronauts Gone Wild'* was a follow-up to his prior documentary titled *'A Funny Thing Happened on the Way to the Moon'* (also available on youtube).

In this film, Sibrel purportedly obtained classified footage showing that the Apollo 11 footage of earth from space was faked.

Beginning at the 33:37 mark of the video, Apollo 11 astronauts are shown staging footage of the earth through a circular window of the 'spacecraft'. Sibrel claims that the film was 'nuclear-dated' and shown to be filmed the day before the astronauts purportedly landed on the moon, making an actual trip to the moon an impossibility.

When confronted with that footage in the follow-up movie *'Astronauts Gone Wild'*, the astronauts don't deny its legitimacy.

At the 8:58 mark of *'Astronauts Gone Wild'*, Buzz Aldrin, thought to be the second person to ever step foot on the moon, lashes out at Sibrel after viewing the footage and seemingly forgetting that a camera was recording his response:

And this makes you a real famous person for having discovered all this. What an ego you must have to want to propel yourself like this.

Octonauts

All space walks are *rehearsed* in gigantic swimming pools, equipped with *"full scale working models"* of the International Space Station.

A 2004 nasa.gov article titled *'Astronauts Take a Dive'* describes the swimming pools used to simulate **all** NASA space missions:

*Why do astronauts need to know how to swim? After all, **there's no water in space**. There is water on Earth, though, and much of the practice for **space walks takes place underwater**. Astronauts dive to the bottom of a 12-meter- (40-foot-) deep tank called the Neutral Buoyancy Laboratory (NBL) because it simulates conditions very close to the weightlessness of space.*

*Anyone who's ever swum knows that your body works very differently underwater. Heavy objects move with ease, and your body feels light and tends to drift and float. This is similar to how it feels to be in the microgravity of space. This is a great way for astronauts to simulate activities. **Every experiment or project that will be used while onboard the Space Shuttle or International Space Station (ISS) is tested underwater before it goes into space. Extra-Vehicular Activities (EVAs),*** *also called space walks, are practiced underwater. Any task to be done in space will be rehearsed several times in the NBL. Practice makes perfect, and when the environment is as uncertain as space, it's a good idea to log as many practice hours as possible. There are several NBLs in the United States and Russia, but the majority of astronaut preparations take place at the facility at Johnson Space Center in Texas.*

Picture a large, indoor swimming pool. An Olympic-sized pool is 50 meters (160 feet) long. The NBL is 61.5 m (202 ft) long, 31 m (102 ft) wide, 12.1 m (40 ft) deep, and holds 234,650,000 liters (6.2 million gallons) of water. An Olympic-sized pool holds about 957,600 liters (253,000 gallons). The water is kept between 27 and 30 °Celsius (82-86 °Fahrenheit), and is recycled every 19.6 hours. The NBL is substantially larger than a large swimming pool, which stands to reason, given the large objects placed inside.

Full-scale working models of the Space Shuttle and ISS robotic arms fit inside the NBL. This allows astronauts to practice any necessary maneuvers before they head into orbit. The fully constructed Space Station will be too large to fit inside, but all modules and experiment areas will easily fit in the pool. The full team of astronauts, suited up in modified space suits, may work on any given project. They are accompanied by a team of divers to help with any logistical issues that may arise. Voice communication systems are installed in the pool and in the space suits. Support staff on dry land can interact and advise the astronauts as their training proceeds.

The article describes how the "*astronauts*" perform the exact same tasks as they do in 'space':

Astronauts perform many tasks in the NBL, from repairing the Hubble Space Telescope, to maintaining the exterior functions of the ISS, to installing new hardware.

For research and training purposes, the space-swims are filmed (the article continues):

*Besides the water facilities, the NBL features **a control room with a variety of computerized monitoring devices so that the astronauts' training can be filmed** and evaluated. It also allows for robots to be controlled and other interactive devices to be operated.*

Space agencies tell us that there is no water in space, though some of the astronauts may disagree with that assessment.

A December 2015 article published on universetoday.com describes an interesting and unknown phenomenon which caused an astronaut to nearly drown while in *'space'*.

The article, titled *'As Astronaut's Helmet Filled With Water, He Told NASA 3 Times It Wasn't From Drinking Bag'*, describes a 2013 *"spacewalk"* gone terribly wrong:

*While NASA's Mission Control **"performed admirably"** during a spacewalk **water leak crisis** in July, a report on the incident showed that controllers did not send astronaut Luca Parmitano back to the airlock until after **he made three calls saying the water didn't appear to be from a drinking bag.***

The report found that *"no aging problem was detected"* from the 35-year old space suit, the astronaut who nearly drowned describes a *"leak"* in his suit, though he *"**softened his stance**"* **after controllers spoke with him:**

Parmitano warned controllers multiple times. *The transcript shows three separate calls from Parmitano saying it wasn't the drinking bag at cause: (1) "I feel a lot of water **on the back of my head**, but I don't think it is from my bag." (2) **"The leak is not from the water bag and it is increasing."** (3) "I'm thinking that it might not be the water bag." (In between 1 and 2, he also sent another call saying his "only guess" was it was the drinking bag, but the report adds that Parmitano may have*

softened his stance after speaking to controllers). *Misunderstanding about the severity, lack of training, "**cognitive overload**" of controllers, and space-to-ground-to-space communication difficulties are all cited as contributing factors.*

While there is no water in space and astronauts are said to be in completely air-tight spacesuits, there are numerous '*actual*' filmed missions – by NASA and other 'space agencies' - which show air bubbles mysteriously rising through 'the vacuum of space'.

China has also been accused of filming their space missions in a swimming pool. A 2008 article published on theepochtimes.com titled '*Chinese Space Walk Filmed in Water, Say Chinese Bloggers*' explains:

*Chinese state-run media called the Shenzhou VII mission "a historic moment." However, online bloggers have pointed out **physics-defying phenomena** in the news footage of its space walk that suggest the whole operation was **filmed not in space, but under water**.*

It would seem that **all** space agencies 'simulate' their space missions in swimming pools.

In 2014, Russian scientists working for Roscosmos (Russia's 'space agency') claim to have found *"sea plankton"* growing outside of the International Space Station.

An article published on theguardian.com titled '*Sea plankton have been found on the International Space Station – but how did they get there?*' attempts to explain this *bizarre* anomaly:

*This, the agency writes, confirms "that some organisms can live on the surface of the International Space Station (ISS) for years amid factors of a space flight, such as zero gravity, temperature conditions and hard cosmic radiation. **Several surveys** proved that these organisms can even develop."*

*Stuff website reported that the plankton samples "were not carried there at launch, but are thought to **have been blown over by air currents on Earth**".*

A 2006 NPR.org article titled '*Inside Russia's space camp*' takes a look inside Russia's "Star City" astronaut training compound. "Star City" still resembles a top-secret military compound, with a massive pool used for 'space' simulations:

*These days, Star City has very advanced training equipment, **including a pool, which is capable of taking a 20 tonne space capsule, for simulating weightlessness.***

"The American people don't believe anything's real until they see it on television." – Richard Nixon; 37th U.S. President

In **1968**, the groundbreaking movie '*2001: A Space Odyssey*' was released. Written by Stanley Kubrick and Arthur C. Clarke, and directed by Stanley Kubrick, the film was nominated for four Academy Awards, and won the Academy Award for *Best Visual Effects*.

A 2013 Space.com article titled '*Stanley Kubrick's Iconic '2001: A Space Odyssey' Sci-Fi Film Explained*' explains the significance of the film:

The production design of "2001" ***heavily influenced the look of space travel*** *in sci-fi films* ***and television for decades****. Kubrick's* ***techniques for filming model spacecraft led to the computerized camera-control methods pioneered in "Star Wars" 10 years later.***

The timing of the film, coupled with Kubrick's gift for making space travel appear real, cause some to suspect that **Kubrick was a key player in the 'moon landing hoax'**.

Something's Fishy

(photo taken with a fisheye lens)

The **fisheye lens**, also referred to as the whole eye, wide-eye, and wide-angle lens, causes things that aren't curved to appear so.

A howstuffworks.com article titled '*What is fisheye lens photography?*' describes what makes a fisheye lens so unique:

*Straight lines anywhere but dead center in the fisheye image appear to curve. The farther they are from center, **the greater the curved distortion**. This offers fun artistic avenues to explore, but it's also very useful.*

*Whereas a rectilinear lens is designed to behave like a window as light moves as straight as possible through its series of elements, the fisheye lens uses its **elements like a funnel, bending a wide angle of light** captured by the extremely curved outer element of the lens toward the film or sensor inside the camera. **The fisheye's signature distortion comes from this funnel-shaped path: Light at the edges of the frame has to bend further to reach the film or sensor, resulting in greater distortion** [sources: Atkins; Kingslake].*

The article proceeds to describe how **any** digital image can be distorted to appear curved:

*The digital photography revolution means you can achieve the fisheye effect without owning one of these unique lenses. Most **photo editing*** *software programs offer a "spherization" filter, which **essentially distorts a square image into a circular shape**. While this won't let you capture the extremely wide angle-of-view of a true fisheye lens, it's an easy way to give your digital photos a different look.*

This distortion is demonstrated in the 2014 youtube documentary 'GoPro: Red Bull Stratos – the Full Story'.

The documentary follows daredevil Felix Baumgartner as he purportedly ascends 24 miles high in a "*stratospheric balloon*," and jumps back down to earth with a GoPro camera -which utilizes a fisheye lens - filming a first-person view of the fall.

At the 2:15 mark of the documentary, Baumgartner opens the hatch, revealing the earth as a flat plane. Once he exits the capsule, the fisheye lens distortion becomes apparent.

Beginning at the 4:05 mark of the documentary, the lens shows the earth bending one way, then the other, clearly demonstrating that the footage is not an accurate depiction of the shape of the earth.

Nevertheless, people accept **this type of footage** as confirmation that the earth is a spherical.

My Dog Ate ~~My Homework~~ the Moon Tapes

An examination of visual evidence of past space mission —most notably the first one ever - would provide valuable information.

Unfortunately, the original footage of the Apollo 11 moon landing is no longer available, as it was *mistakenly* erased.

A 2009 NPR.org article titled *'Houston, We Erased The Apollo 11 Tapes'* explains the unfortunate oversight:

*An exhaustive, three-year search for some tapes that contained the original footage of the Apollo 11 moonwalk has concluded that they were probably destroyed during a period when **NASA was erasing old magnetic tapes and reusing them to record satellite data.***

"We're all saddened that they're not there. We all wish we had 20-20 hindsight," says Dick Nafzger, a TV specialist at NASA's Goddard Space Flight Center in Maryland, who helped lead the search team.

*"**I don't think anyone in the NASA organization did anything wrong,**" Nafzger says. "I think it **slipped through the cracks**, and nobody's happy about it."*

*NASA has, however, **offered up a consolation prize** for the 40th anniversary of the Apollo 11 mission — the agency has taken the best available broadcast television footage and contracted with a digital restoration firm to enhance it, so that the public can see the first moonwalk in more detail than ever before.*

NASA has been careless with much of this *historical* material. A 2011 report on Space.com titled, *'NASA Has Lost Hundreds of Its Moon Rocks, New Report Says'*, describes how many *priceless* moon rocks have turned up missing:

NASA has lost or misplaced more than 500 of the moon rocks its Apollo astronauts collected and brought back to Earth, according to a new agency report.

In an audit released Thursday (Dec. 8), NASA's Office of Inspector General states that the agency **"lacks sufficient controls over its loans of moon rocks and other astromaterials, which increases the risk that these unique resources may be lost."**

It turns out that these *"unique resources"* may not be so unique after all. Shortly after the Apollo 11 mission, the astronauts started handing out fake moon rocks.

A 2009 article on the telegraph.co.uk titled, *''Moon rock' given to Holland by Neil Armstrong and Buzz Aldrin is fake :A moon rock given to the Dutch prime minister by Apollo 11 astronauts in 1969 has turned out to be a fake'* describes one incident:

*Curators at Amsterdam's Rijksmuseum, where the rock has attracted tens of thousands of visitors each year, discovered that the "lunar rock", valued at £308,000, **was in fact petrified wood**.*

It did not take long for those with a trained eye to see that the rocks were terrestrial in nature (the article continues):

*Researchers Amsterdam's Free University **were able to tell at a glance** that the rock was unlikely to be from the moon, a **conclusion that was borne out by tests**.*

*"It's a nondescript, pretty-much-**worthless stone**," said Frank Beunk, a geologist involved in the investigation.*

After Neil Armstrong passed away, his wife found a bag full of equipment taken on the 'first moon mission'. In 2015, a cnn.com article titled *'Neil Armstrong's widow finds artifacts from moonwalk in a closet'* describes the discovery and the lack of oversight regarding these *valuable* pieces of history:

*Inside the **bag was the camera that recorded Armstrong's landing on the moon, as well as his famous remarks upon his landing**. The 16mm data acquisition camera was mounted in the window of the lunar module Eagle and recorded historic images: Armstrong just before he stepped onto the moon. Armstrong planting the American flag with Buzz Aldrin.*

Also a part of the haul was a waist tether used by Armstrong to help support his feet during a rest period on the moon. Astronauts used these tethers as security in case they were forced to do a spacewalk during orbit, the museum release said.

Nevertheless, the legend of the moon landings still lives on, along with the infamous Neil Armstrong quote recited as a great milestone of human achievement:

"That's one small step for man, one giant leap for mankind."

Seeing is ~~Not~~ Believing

The current visual evidence of 'space' is digital, which comes with a host of concerns.

For legal purposes, visual digital evidence is known to be *easily manipulated.*

A publication on the American Bar Association's website, americanbar.org, describes the problems with digital evidence:

*As a consequence, digital displays also have a greater likelihood of drawing objections **due to the ease** at which they can be: (1) **manipulated and altered** using photo enhancement software or other novel techniques not used with traditional analog photos; (2) **degraded, tampered with, or edited** (e.g., as to resolution, sound, or frames in a digital video); and (3) **interpreted differently by simply changing data** (e.g., viewpoints, angles, or lighting in a computer display).*

We trust that the images of the earth and space are real, but the fact that most are admittedly compilations is little-known.

The most popular image of the earth, which serves as the iphone default home-page image, is a compilation. In a 2011 gizmodo.com article titled '*The Secrets Behind the Most Famous Earth Image of All Time*', we learn how 'the pros' *create* the images which most people *assume* are real:

*Unlike Apollo 17's photograph of the whole Earth, NASA's Blue Marble is **not a real photograph. It's a composite made of many other images.***

*Simmon created the image using a 43,200-pixel by 21,600-pixel map of the Earth stitched together by Reto Stöckli. **Stöckli used about ten***

66

thousand 300-megabyte satellite scenes captured by the Terra satellite over a period of 100 days. *(Back then, Terra was NASA's latest Earth-monitoring satellite.)* **Stöckli took out all the clouds and left that huge image clean.** Then Simmon came in and **added some details:** "**To make the Earth look realistic, or at least how I imagined the Earth would look, I needed to do some work.**"

There he **mapped them onto a sphere, rendering separate images for everything:** "land and ocean, specular highlight, clouds, a couple day/night masks, and atmospheric haze".

He finally **brought these images into Photoshop and combined them for hours,** "tweaking and re-tweaking transparency, layer masks, hue, saturation, gaussian blur, and curves to get an image that looked **like the picture I had in my head.**" The result is beautiful. **<u>A sweet, beautiful lie.</u>**

A 2015 nationalgeorgraphic.com article titled '*NASA's 'Blue Marbles': Pictures of Earth From 1972 to Today*' describes how NASA finally released an *actual* image of earth; the first actual image in 43 years:

On Monday, NASA released a photo of the entire sunlit side of Earth— **the first since the original Blue Marble photo in 1972.**

The 1972 photo, which was taken on the Apollo 17 mission, the last 'manned mission to the moon', was reportedly taken from 28,000 miles away. The 2015 image was purportedly taken from over *one million miles away.*

(1972 on the left; 2015 on the right; courtesy of NASA)

In 2012, the 'composite' image of the United States appears about twice as large as the 2002 composite:

(2002 and 2012; images courtesy of NASA)

While this discrepancy is cause for concern, we are informed that people simply have a *"misunderstanding about how the photos are taken."* A 2015 article on metabunk.org titled *'Debunked: "Blue Marble" Photos show a Changing Earth'* explains:

*Some more **extreme theorists** have suggested that the image is fake because the continents (particularly North America) appear to be a different size to earlier photos.*

The misconception comes from a misunderstanding about how the photos are taken. *This new 2015 image is noteworthy because it's the first time since 1972 that a good quality single image photograph has been taken of the Earth. The previous last image (in 1972) was taken by an astronaut from on board the Apollo 17 spacecraft during the last manned mission to the Moon. This was the first image called the "Blue Marble", although there had been similar images taken before (such as the 1967 images taken by the ATS3 satellite), the 1972 Blue Marble image became iconic, and remains the last such image taken by an actual person.*

For those still unsure, the article continues:

The difference comes down to the way the photos were taken, *and what was done to them after they were taken. In particular, the bright blue 2002 image is* **not a photo at all***. It's a composite image made of many individual photos taken by a very low orbit satellite (Terra). The images were* **stitched together** *in three dimensions, and then various projected images were generated by computer - in much the same way that Google Earth creates images of the globe from multiple satellite images. A similar image was created in 2012 with the NPP Suomi satellite.*

In July of 2016, NASA released images (and video) of the moon passing in front of the earth:

(2016; courtesy of NASA)

The images appear to be fabrications, however NASA backs their authenticity.

In July 2016, the washingtonpost.com published an article titled '*Why NASA's new photos of the moon look super fake (even though they're not)*' to address the concerns.

The article concludes that if indeed the images were faked, NASA surely would have done a better job:

That bright-green contrast makes the dark edge of the moon stand out even more — and frankly looks like **some pretty sloppy Photoshop work in its own right**. One has to hope that if our tax dollars truly were funding some grand space cover-up, NASA would do a slightly better job of fooling us. But hey, space is hard.

'Magnificent' images of all the far-off galaxies and star clusters are just composites as well. A 2015 article on wired.com titled 'The Secrets Behind All Those Gorgeous Photos of Space' describes how all the awe-inspiring images, such as the one below (courtesy of NASA), are also not exactly as they seem:

Astrophotography is far more difficult than simply pointing a lens at the sky. The best photos come from powerful telescopes like the Hubble or Gemini North hooked up to highly specialized cameras. Using the Hubble as an example, scientists aim the telescope toward the expanse of sky they want to explore, with a pointing accuracy of 0.007 arc seconds— which NASA says is like being able to shine a laser on a dime 200 miles away. Incoming light is reflected off a primary mirror almost 8 feet in diameter onto the secondary mirror, which reflects it into the telescopes optical equipment, which includes half a dozen cameras. NASA likes to say the Hubble can see objects with an angular size as small as 0.05 arc seconds, which is like being in Washington, DC, and spotting two fireflies in Tokyo. The telescope captures images in monochromatic grayscale. Filters sensitive to specific wavelengths of light recreate color; **the final images that amaze us are composites.**

Check out this Cool Video, Dude!

One would assume that there must be overwhelming video evidence showing the entire earth spinning on its axis. With thousands of 'satellites' circling the 'globe', and the International Space Station constantly orbiting overhead, the video evidence should be overwhelming.

But there is none.

A 2011 article on dailymail.co.uk titled *'Amazing video of the Earth spinning taken from the International Space Station'* describes how the *"amazing video"* is actually just a video collage of still images:

*This is **one film** that's sure to leave you in a spin.*

*The crew of the International Space Station **pointed a camera at North America and the resulting still pictures were spliced together** into a mesmerising speeded-up sequence.*

It shows a rotation of the Earth in just a matter of seconds from a vantage point 225 miles up.

In 2014, NASA decided to live-stream footage (on ustream.tv) of the earth from the International Space Station. NASA describes the feature:

*Live video from the International Space Station includes internal views when the crew is on-duty and Earth views at other times. The video is accompanied by audio of conversations between the crew and Mission Control. **This video is only available when the space station is in contact with the ground. During "loss of signal" periods, viewers will see a blue screen.***

*Since the station orbits the Earth once every 90 minutes, it experiences a sunrise or a sunset about every 45 minutes. When the station is in darkness, **external camera video may appear black**, but can sometimes provide spectacular views of lightning or city lights below.*

Live streaming footage should be convincing evidence of a spinning global earth, but the footage underwhelms and provides little substance.

One cause for concern is that the live-feed is not continuous. With modern technology and NASA's budget, a continuous live-feed should be easily achievable.

Also, the live-feed only captures the top portion of the earth; the high tech cameras are seemingly unable to zoom-out far enough to capture a full view of our 'spinning globe'.

A July 2016 article on Space.com titled *'Watch Earth Spin Through a Full Year in This Spectacular Time-Lapse Video'* also sounds as though actual video footage will be shown, but instead it's another compilation:

Talk about "As the World Turns": A sped-up video of Earth spinning through space shows a dizzying array of clouds and continents from a satellite located 1 million miles (1.6 million kilometers) away.

*The time-lapse video of 3,000 images shows **pictures taken** every 2 hours. The pictures come courtesy of the EPIC camera on the Deep Space Climate Observatory (DSCOVR) satellite. The satellite is located at a gravitationally stable spot in space between the Earth and the sun known as a Lagrange point.*

The footage of astronauts floating around the International Space Station and giving interviews from space should prove the ball-earth case, but that's not the case.

All of 'space' footage can be easily filmed on earth.

Zero-gravity airplanes simulate the 'weightlessness of space' by descending rapidly. Coincidentally, NASA uses these planes for 'simulation purposes-only'.

In a 2004 article titled *'Zero-Gravity Plane on Final Flight'*, NASA describes the process while paying homage to a decommissioned plane:

*Astronaut candidates are **required to fly in the microgravity program as part of their training**. Engineers test equipment and procedures designed for spaceflight. Scientists do basic research on board. **Some scenes from the movie "Apollo 13" were filmed on a NASA KC-135A**. The plane typically flies four days a week.*

Zero-gravity simulation flights are available to civilians as well. A 2004 article on nbcnews.com titled '*Zero-gravity flights go mainstream*' provides insight regarding the logistics:

*Passengers aboard the modified Boeing 727-200 jet will experience weightlessness for **about 25 seconds at a time**, courtesy of the plane's special parabolic flight path. The physics behind the experience is analogous to what happens during a roller-coaster ride or a fast elevator descent. But inside the jet's padded passenger cabin, **fliers are able to tumble in the air or do a "Superman" fly-through, similar to the acrobatics performed on the international space station.***

*Such flights have **long been available for researchers and astronauts from NASA** and the French company Novespace, and the Russians took parabolic flight one step further by allowing tourists to buy rides on similarly outfitted IL-76 cargo jets.*

Many movies demonstrate the fact that 'space' is easily faked in Hollywood studios.

The 2013 sci-fi move Ender's Game, a 2013 sci-fi movie starring Harrison Ford, had extensive zero-gravity action scenes.

Orson Scott Card, the author of the Ender's Game book, was on-location to make a cameo appearance in the film.

In a 2012 article on slashfilms.com titled '*Orson Scott Card Describes Zero Gravity Scenes From Set Of 'Ender's Game;' Reveals Cameo*', Card describes how zero-gravity footage is manufactured for movies:

*Stunt coordinator Garrett Warren took what he learned from the weightless work he did on **Avatar** built on it.*

*There is a mechanism used for training gymnasts – **a wheel they wear around their waists that allows them to rotate in space while suspended from wires. Warren used this on Avatar, which allows a great deal of apparent freedom of movement in space – once the computer artists have erased the wheel rig, you can't tell that there's any way a wire could have been attached.***

*But this is only the beginning. The illusion of freefall depends on the **actors' moving correctly**. Where gravity naturally draws their limbs downward, in zero-gravity the arms and legs and heads continue in the direction of the last movement, until something stops them.*

*And they have the strength and training to do constant **movements and poses that defy gravity, without ever looking as if they're working hard.***

*Fitted with the wheel rigs, they were being **moved through space like puppets – and at every moment, they had to make sure their "nonvolitional" movements followed the rules of inertia-driven** rather than gravity-driven motion.*

*It was agonizing. Human muscles aren't meant to work like that. **And Warren was watching everything, playing it back again and again, catching any false movements.***

The Mars 'Missions'

Mars, also known as "the red planet," has been a *prime* space destination for over 50 years.

Beginning in 1960, there have been 46 different unmanned missions to Mars, according to NASA. While some of these 'missions' fail at launch, the vast majority are recorded as being successful.

Depending on our respective orbits, Mars and earth are purportedly between 34 million and 250 million miles apart – give or take a *few million miles.*

We are told that 'spacecrafts', using the same propulsion methods used in the Apollo missions, are able to travel millions of miles through space in order to send high-quality images back to earth.

A 2012 article on Space.com titled *'How Far Away is Mars'* explains how the 'missions to Mars' have been occurring since before the advent of cell phones and color TVs, in an efficient and *environmentally-friendly* manner:

*In their race around the sun, Earth on its inside track laps Mars every 26 months. This close approach provides an opportunity — a launch window — to send spacecraft to the red planet. Rather than pointing the spacecraft at Mars, engineers aim it in a wide orbit around the sun. The sun's gravity gives the spacecraft a boost — **called a gravity assist or slingshot effect —saving time and fuel**. The spacecraft's orbit then intersects with Mars.*

In an article titled *'Sibling Rivalry: A Mars/Earth Comparison'*, NASA describes the striking similarities between Mars and earth:

Scientific understanding is often a matter of making the right comparisons. In terms of studying the Earth, one of the **best comparative laboratories** exists one planet over -- on Mars. In many ways, the study of **Mars provides Earth-bound scientists with a control set** as they look at the processes of climate change, geophysics, and the potential for life beyond our own planet.

Not everyone is buying the official story. A November 2016 article on scienceworldreport.com titled '*Hoax Claims NASA Faked Mars Rover Landing*' describes a one of the *"conspiracy theories"*:

*There have been plenty of conspiracy theories and hoax news regarding NASA's projects and studies. But so-called **Mars "truthers"** are now claiming that the space agency did not actually send the rover to Mars but rather it has been **filming footage here on Earth**, specifically, on Devon Island in Canada.*

"The Space Agency" acknowledges that the terrain on Mars just happens to look the same as certain regions on earth, but the connection is *merely a coincidence*:

*For their part, Express UK noted that **the Space Agency** did admit that the large, uninhabited island **"resembles the Mars surface in more ways than any other place on Earth."** They also insisted that their **base at Nunavut, Devon Island, which they had since 1997, is a means to practice for real Mars expeditions, as the Haughton Crater provides the perfect terrain for such a job**.*

Those who are skeptical should *"rest assured"* that the experts **would never lie** (the article concludes):

*Rest assured, Professor Lewis Dartnell of the University of Westminster said that NASA's Mars rover program is real. "The radio signals beamed back to Earth from Opportunity and Curiosity are picked up by an international system of radio dishes called the Deep Space Network -- so if this was a conspiracy then **many different nations would need to be involved**, and not just the USA."*

Humans to Mars!

*"I want Americans to win the race for the kinds of discoveries that unleash new jobs . . . pushing out into the solar system not just to visit, **but to stay**," the president said. "Last month, we launched a new spacecraft as part of a **re-energized space program that will send American astronauts to Mars**."* – Former U.S. President Barack Obama; January, 2015 State of the Union Address

With their 'official' 2016 budget approaching $20 billion, NASA keeps the story moving, with the help of politicians, media, and 'science'.

In February 2015, the 2016 NASA budget of $18.5 billion was proposed (and subsequently approved).

NASA administrator Charlie Bolden describes NASA's bold vision for the future (on NASA.gov):

*"Today, President Obama is proposing an additional $18.5 billion for NASA, **building on the significant investments the administration has made in America's space program over the past six years**," Bolden said. "**NASA is firmly on a journey to Mars**. Make no mistake, this journey will help guide and define our generation."*

Bolden noted that the budget allows NASA to continue development of the Orion crew vehicle, Space Launch System and Exploration Ground

*Systems that will **<u>one day</u> send astronauts beyond low-Earth orbit...***

*During 2014, NASA continued several highly successful missions highlighted by the maiden flight of Orion. The spacecraft completed its first voyage to space, **traveling farther than any spacecraft designed for astronauts in more than 40 years.***

Black Budget

In addition to NASA's official budget, it appears that some of the unaccounted-for 'Black Budget' monies make their way into 'space'-related endeavors as well.

A 2014 article on thedailybeast.com titled '*Read the Pentagon's $59 Billion 'Black Budget'* describes the decception:

The term is an unofficial one, as shadowy as the thing that it seeks to describe. The Washington Post used it to describe the Snowden-leaked account of money that funds Central Intelligence Agency, National Security Agency, and other spy service projects, known officially as the National Intelligence Program (NIP). It can also refer to the Department of Defense's Military Intelligence Program (MIP). The MIP as we know it was established in 2005 and includes all the intelligence programs that support operations in armed services.

Think spy satellites, stealth bombers, next-missile-spotting radars, next-gen drones, and ultra-powerful eavesdropping gear. *Think projects to size up the Russian army and snoop on Kim Jung-Un's nuclear program.*

Satellites

(Jason-2 satellite; 'image' courtesy of NASA)

Satellites are a crucial aspect of the 'space' story, with thousands of these crafts purportedly just outside earth's atmosphere.

In a 2014 nasa.gov article titled *'What is a Satellite'*, NASA profiles these technological wonders:

A satellite is a moon, planet or machine that orbits a planet or star. For example, Earth is a satellite because it orbits the sun. Likewise, the moon is a satellite because it orbits Earth. Usually, the word "satellite" refers to a machine that is launched into space and moves around Earth or another body in space.

*Earth and the moon are examples of **natural satellites. Thousands** of artificial, or man-made, satellites orbit Earth. Some take pictures of the planet that help meteorologists predict weather and track hurricanes. Some take pictures of other planets, the sun, black holes, dark matter or faraway galaxies. These pictures help scientists better understand the solar system and universe.*

Still other satellites are used mainly for communications, such as beaming TV signals and phone calls around the world. A group of more than 20 satellites make up the Global Positioning System, or GPS. If you have a GPS receiver, these satellites can help figure out your exact location.

Why Are Satellites Important?
The bird's-eye view that satellites have allows them to see <u>large areas</u> of Earth at one time. This ability means satellites can collect more data, more quickly, than instruments on the ground.

Satellites also can see into space better than telescopes at Earth's surface. That's because satellites fly above the clouds, dust and molecules in the atmosphere that can block the view from ground level.

Before satellites, TV signals didn't go very far. TV signals only travel in straight lines. So **they would quickly trail off into space instead of following Earth's curve.** Sometimes mountains or tall buildings would block them. Phone calls to faraway places were also a problem. **Setting up telephone wires over long distances or underwater is difficult and costs a lot.**

With satellites, **TV signals and phone calls are sent upward to a satellite. Then, almost instantly, the satellite can send them back down to different locations on Earth.**

What Are the Parts of a Satellite?
Satellites come in many shapes and sizes. But most have at least two parts in common - an antenna and a power source. **The antenna sends and receives information,** often to and from Earth. The **power source can be a solar panel or battery.** Solar panels make power by turning sunlight into electricity.

Many NASA satellites carry cameras and scientific sensors. **Sometimes these instruments point toward Earth** to gather information about its land, air and water. **Other times they face toward space** to collect data *from the solar system and universe.*

How Do Satellites Orbit Earth?

*Most satellites are launched into space on rockets. A satellite orbits Earth when its speed is **balanced by the pull of Earth's gravity**. Without this balance, the satellite would fly in a straight line off into space or fall back to Earth. Satellites orbit Earth at different heights, different speeds and along different paths. The two most common types of orbit are "**geostationary**" (jee-oh-STAY-shun-air-ee) and "**polar.**"*

*A **geostationary satellite travels from west to east over the equator. It moves in the same direction and at the same rate Earth is spinning**. From Earth, **a geostationary satellite looks like it is standing still** since it is **always above the same location.***

*Polar-orbiting satellites travel in a north-south direction from pole to pole. As Earth spins underneath, these satellites can scan the entire globe, **one strip at a time.***

Why Don't Satellites Crash Into Each Other?

***Actually, they can**. NASA and other U.S. and international organizations keep track of satellites in space. **Collisions are rare** because when a satellite is launched, it is placed into an orbit **designed to avoid other satellites**. But orbits can change over time. And the chances of a crash increase as more and more satellites are launched into space.*

*In February 2009, two communications satellites - one American and one Russian - collided in space. This, **however**, is believed to be the first time two man-made satellites have collided accidentally.*

What Was the First Satellite in Space?

Sputnik 1 was the first satellite in space. The Soviet Union launched it in 1957.

What Is the History of NASA Satellites?

NASA has launched dozens of satellites into space, starting with the **Explorer 1 satellite in 1958. Explorer 1 was America's first man-made satellite. The main instrument aboard was a sensor that measured high-energy particles in space called cosmic rays.**

The first satellite picture of Earth came from NASA's Explorer 6 in 1959. TIROS-1 followed in 1960 with the first TV picture of Earth from space. **These pictures did not show much detail.** But they did show the potential satellites had to **change how people view Earth and space.**

How Does NASA Use Satellites Today?

NASA satellites help scientists study Earth and space.

Satellites looking toward Earth provide information about clouds, oceans, land and ice. They also measure gases in the atmosphere, such as ozone and carbon dioxide, and the amount of energy that Earth absorbs and emits. **And satellites monitor wildfires, volcanoes and their smoke.**

All this information helps scientists predict weather and climate. The information also helps public health officials track disease and famine; it helps farmers know what crops to plant; and it helps emergency workers respond to natural disasters.

Satellites that face toward space have a variety of jobs. Some watch for dangerous rays coming from the sun. Others explore asteroids and comets, the history of stars, and the origin of planets. **Some satellites fly near or orbit other planets. These spacecraft may look for evidence of water on Mars or capture close-up pictures of Saturn's rings.**

Space Junk

(*Space junk; courtesy of NASA*)

As a result of all the artificial satellites which have been launched since 1960, an excessive amount of 'space junk' now whizzes aimlessly through 'space', posing big problems, according to NASA.

A 2013 article on nasa.gov titled '*Space Debris and Human Spacecraft*' describes the problems, and NASA's will to overcome them:

*More than 500,000 pieces of debris, or "space junk," **are tracked** as they orbit the Earth. They all travel at **speeds up to 17,500 mph,** fast enough for a relatively small piece of orbital debris to damage a satellite or a spacecraft.*

*The rising population of space debris increases the **potential danger to all space vehicles**, but especially to the International Space Station, space shuttles and other spacecraft with humans aboard.*

The size of the space junk varies, with millions of pieces purportedly undetected as they whiz around the earth (the article continues):

*There are more than 20,000 pieces of debris larger than a softball orbiting the Earth. They travel at speeds up to 17,500 mph, fast enough for a relatively small piece of orbital debris to damage a satellite or a spacecraft. **There are 500,000 pieces of debris the size of a marble or larger. There are many millions of pieces of debris that are so small they can't be tracked.***

Despite the abundance of deadly junk flying around at *8 miles per second*, NASA has kept the ISS and the astronauts safe. By utilizing a *"pizza box"* protocol, employing *"debris avoidance maneuver"* practices, and keeping various *aces in the hole* for last minute emergencies, *"Mission Control"* has an impeccable safety track record (the article continues):

Planning for and Reacting to Debris

NASA has a set of long-standing guidelines that are used to assess whether the threat of such a close pass is sufficient to warrant evasive action or other precautions to ensure the safety of the crew.

*These guidelines essentially draw an imaginary box, known as the "**pizza box**" because of its flat, rectangular shape, around the space vehicle. This box is about a mile deep by 30 miles across by 30 miles long (1.5 x 50 x 50 kilometers), with the vehicle in the center. When predictions indicate that the debris will pass close enough for concern and the quality of the tracking data is deemed sufficiently accurate, Mission Control centers in Houston and Moscow work together to develop a prudent course of action.*

*Sometimes these encounters are known well in advance and there is time to move the station slightly, known as a "**debris avoidance maneuver**" to keep the debris outside of the box. Other times, the tracking data isn't precise enough to warrant such a maneuver or the* close pass isn't identified in time to make the maneuver. In those cases, the control centers may agree that the best course of action is to **move the crew into the Soyuz spacecraft** that are used to transport humans to and from the station. This allows enough time to isolate those spaceships from the station by **closing hatches** in the event of a damaging collision. The crew would be able to leave the station if the collision caused a loss of pressure in the life-supporting module or damaged critical components. The Soyuz act as lifeboats for crew members in the event of an emergency.

Mission Control also has the option of taking additional precautions, such as closing hatches between some of the station's modules, if the likelihood of a collision is great enough.

Maneuvering Spacecraft to Avoid Orbital Debris

NASA has a set of long-standing guidelines that are used to assess whether the threat of a close approach of orbital debris to a spacecraft is sufficient to warrant evasive action or precautions to ensure the safety of the crew.

Debris avoidance maneuvers are planned when the probability of collision from a conjunction reaches limits set in the space shuttle and space station flight rules. **If the probability of collision is greater than 1 in 100,000, a maneuver will be conducted if it will not result in significant impact to mission objectives. If it is greater than 1 in 10,000, a maneuver will be conducted unless it will result in additional risk to the crew.**

Debris avoidance maneuvers are usually small and occur from one to several hours before the time of the conjunction. Debris avoidance maneuvers with the shuttle can be planned and executed in a matter of hours. **Such maneuvers with the space station require about 30 hours**

to plan and execute mainly due to the need to use the station's Russian thrusters, or the propulsion systems on one of the docked Russian or European spacecraft.

Several collision avoidance maneuvers with the shuttle and the station have been conducted during the past 10 years.

A Costly Endeavor

Satellites are big business. Globalcom Satellite Communications (globalcomsatphone.com), provider of 'satellite' internet and phone services, describes the astronomical costs associated with the satellite 'business' in an article titled '*The Cost of Building and Launching a Satellite*':

*Satellites are not cheap business. They cost a lot of money to design, construct, launch and monitor. Just how much money? If you **have at least $290 million** in your bank account, that money can go into making a satellite that can track and monitor hurricanes. **Add about $100 million dollars more** if you want a satellite that carries a missile-warning device.*

What makes satellites so expensive?
*Some of the factors that drive the cost of satellites are the equipment and materials used to build them. Transponders alone hundreds of thousands of dollars a year **to maintain**, while bandwidth cost per MHz is priced at a minimum of about $3,500 a month. **Running a satellite at a 36MHz bandwidth will cost over $1.5 million a year. There are also the other gadgets and equipment that have to be built into the satellite in order for it to perform its intended function. These can include computers, computer software and cameras.***

*Another factor that contributes to the expense associated with satellites is the cost of putting one into orbit. It is estimated that a single satellite launch can range in cost from a low of about **$50 million to a high of about $400 million**. Launching a space shuttle mission can **easily cost $500 million dollars**, although one mission is capable of carrying multiple satellites and send them into orbit.*

Also to be considered in the cost of satellites is its **maintenance**. After getting one into orbit, it has to be monitored from a ground facility, **which will require manpower. Satellites are also not impervious to damage or down times**. Furthermore, if things don't go too well during a launch, a multi-million endeavor can either end up in pieces or sustain damages that will cost more money to repair.

Some of the top satellite firms in the U.S. are Hughes, Boeing, Ball Aerospace & Technologies Corp. and Lockheed Martin.

Risky Business

With so much money at stake, insurance figures prominently into the equation.

Spaceco, which is a subsidiary of insurance company Allianz (allianz.com), appears to be one of the only, if not **the only**, companies providing 'space insurance'.

In their 'Covering Satellite Risks' assessment, unique offerings are described:

Space risk management is a very complex discipline. It combines contract analysis and advice, risk evaluation, modeling, insurance program design and implementation, alternative risk transfer concepts, as well as claim negotiation. This meshes well with the integration of SpaceCo into AGCS, **which may be the only insurer able to provide the space industry with all lines of business** such as property, liability, marine, aviation, alternative risk transfer and dedicated space insurance. Therefore, insurers have to assure a high level of expertise.

The article continues to describe the costs and risks associated with the 'satellite industry':

There are about **20 to 30 commercial launches every year**. While a big commercial satellite may cost anything between **$300–600m** including its launch, the whole premium for space insurance was estimated at about **$600m** in 2007. As Thierry Colliot puts it, "You can potentially lose the premium of a whole year in one single event."

Consequently, in order to achieve profitability, the principles of coinsurance and the close evaluation of insurable risks are indispensable for SpaceCo. The overall capacity of space insurance markets was

91

*estimated at about **$490m for launch risks and $620m for in-orbit risks in 2007**. The market situation itself, however, **depends mostly on single loss events**.*

The article also provides insight on what these *'commercial satellites'* are used for:

*However, losing a spacecraft is by far not the only risk: potential interruptions of a satellite's service in our globalized world are just as problematic. **This is a huge concern for spacecraft users, individual transponder users such as TV channels and Internet providers, but also for banks, car manufacturers and large industries that use telecommunication networks.***

*Particularly in situations of **tremendous public attention**, for example during broadcasts like **the soccer World Cup Final or the Olympic Games**, a malfunction would prove **disastrous for commercial revenue** and the image of TV stations.*

Feel the ~~Heat~~ Cold

Most satellites, including the Hubble Telescope and the International Space Station, claim to reside in *"low Earth orbit."* This area, known as the thermosphere, is said to reside between 53 and 429 miles from earth.

The thermosphere is below the Van Allen belt, so the 'satellites' purportedly don't have to pass through it. What they do have to contend with though, is extreme heat. The thermosphere can reach 4,500 degrees Fahrenheit (2,400 degrees Celsius), which is above the melting point of all the metals purportedly used in 'satellites'.

Miraculously, a process occurs which doesn't allow the heat to actually be hot. In an article on nasa.gov titled *'The heat that won't keep you warm'*, the rocket scientists at NASA explain the dichotomy:

*The **thermosphere** lies between the exosphere and the mesosphere. "Thermo" means heat, and the temperature in this layer can reach up to **4,500 degrees Fahrenheit**. If you were to hang out in the thermosphere, though, you would be **very cold** because there aren't enough gas molecules to transfer the heat to you. This also means there **aren't enough molecules for sound waves to travel through.***

Interestingly, *"there aren't enough molecules for sound waves to travel through,"* but that doesn't appear to present any communication hurdles between earth and the 'satellites'.

The cameras, which are **sensitive to light, radiation, and temperature changes**, apparently never have any issues and consistently work perfectly.

Transmitting large amounts of data over long distances through the 'void of space' seems to offer no problems either.

NASA purportedly has the technology to seamlessly send data millions of miles; a technology so advanced that even those in high places at NASA don't seem to understand it.

Adam Steltzner, who NASA describes as *"the lead mechanical engineer for the crucial entry, descent and landing events when the rovers reach Mars,"* was stumped when confronted with a question from the press regarding how footage taken on Mars is transmitted back to earth, which is said to be over 140 million miles away (on average):

Question: *"I have to ask you, what type of file-type... Can you tell us about the image file-type and compression that was used to send this very important couple of thumbnails back from Mars?"*

Steltzner's answer: *"Yes, unfortunately **I absolutely cannot**. If Justin Mackie is in the room, or there's a couple other people on the team who would be able to whip that out quickly, but I'm... **I couldn't tell you, sorry.**"*

Steltzner's story is a true success story, showing that anyone can make it if they 'have the right stuff.'

The New York Times reviewed his book, *'The Right Kind of Crazy,'* describing his unique journey:

...from an aspiring musician, who barely graduated from high school, to a California Institute of Technology recruit to a team leader at the J.P.L. in Pasadena, Calif.

The idea of satellites is sexy and cool, but *reality* begs a very important question: why would governments and big-business spend vast fortunes on satellites, when the same objectives can be achieved with a fraction of the cost and almost no risk?

Full of Hot-Air

(public domain image of US blimps near ~~phallus~~ Washington Monument; taken between 1920 and 1932)

When thinking of airships, most commonly referred to as blimps, an image of the Goodyear blimp hovering above the NFL Super Bowl (American football) often comes to mind. Hovering overhead, these airships are seen as cool gimmicks and a place where businesses can advertise.

Airships are also known as blimps, dirigibles, zeppelins, lighter-than-air vehicles, and hybrid airships.

They all have one thing in common: they are **lighter than air.**

The first untethered and manned hot-air balloon flight occurred in 1783.

(painting titled Ascent of the Monsieur Bouclé's Montgolfier Balloon in the Gardens of Aranjuez, 1784)

During the U.S. Civil War (1861 - 1865), hot-air balloons were tethered to the ground and used to scout enemy terrain.

The biggest challenge to consistent high-altitude flights was a reliable steering method, which was solved in the beginning of the 20th century.

The first successful airship was designed by German Graf von Zeppelin in 1900:

The Airlander 10 spans 300 feet (91 meters) with a 30,000 pound cargo load, demonstrating the *evolution* of airships:

(Airlander 10; 2016)

In World War I, German 'Zeppelins' carried out bombing raids, most notably over Paris and England. In a firstworldwar.com article titled *'The War in the Air - Bombers: Germany, Zeppelins'*, the most *"successful"* bombing raid is described:

The most **successful** Zeppelin raid on London in the entire war was on the 8th of September 1915. This raid caused more **than half a million pounds of damage, almost all of it from the one Zeppelin**, the L13, which managed to bomb central London. This single raid caused more than half the material damage caused by all the raids against Britain in 1915.

Following World War I, airships grew in popularity, especially within the United States Navy.

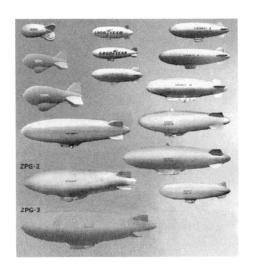

(*image of US Navy and Goodyear airships*)

Due to their supposed ineffectiveness and lack of practicality, interest in these airships seemed to have waned in the following years, with the 1937 'Hindenburg disaster' seemingly signifying the end of an era.

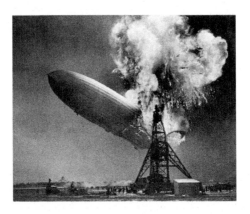

While the common perception is that the airship programs have come and gone, a different picture emerges when you 'follow-the-money'.

Lockheed Martin, a large military-industrial company, demonstrates the *importance* and prevalence of airships in modern society.

On their website, lockheedmartin.com, they describe their '*Lighter Than*

Air Vehicles':

*Lockheed Martin delivered its first Lighter-Than-Air-based **persistent Intelligence, Surveillance and Reconnaissance (ISR) systems** to the U.S. Navy more than 75 years ago. This enduring legacy of Lighter-Than-Air (LTA) innovation, engineering and production has resulted in more than **300 airships and thousands of aerostats** in support of **military operations world-wide**.*

*Lockheed Martin LTA **product line** includes the U.S. Army's Persistent Threat Detection System (PTDS), the U.S. Air Force's Tethered Aerostat Radar System (TARS) and the U.S. Army's unmanned High Altitude Airship (HAA™) currently in development.*

Lockheed Martin goes on to describe their HAA (*High Altitude Airship*) program, which essentially offers "***capabilities on par with satellites at a fraction of the cost***":

*The Lockheed Martin High Altitude Airship (HAA™) – and its sub-scale demonstrator, the High Altitude Long Endurance-Demonstrator (HALE-D) – is an un-tethered, unmanned lighter-than-air vehicle that will operate above the jet stream in a **<u>geostationary position</u>** to deliver persistent station keeping as a **surveillance platform, telecommunications relay, or a weather observer**. The **HAA also provides the Warfighter affordable, ever-present Intelligence, Surveillance and Reconnaissance and rapid communications connectivity over the entire battle space**. The technology is **available now and ready for integration and flight test**.*

*Lockheed Martin and the U.S. Army launched the first-of-its-kinds HALE-D on July 27, 2011, demonstrating key technologies critical to the development of unmanned airships. We demonstrated a variety of **advanced technologies, including launch and control of the airship, communications links, unique propulsion system, solar array electricity generation, remote piloting communications and control capability, and in-flight operations**. High altitude airships can **improve the military's ability to communicate in remote areas such as those in***

Afghanistan, where mountainous terrain frequently interferes with communications signals.

High-strength fabrics to minimize hull weight, thin-film solar arrays for the regenerative power supply, and lightweight propulsion units are key technologies ready to make a high-flying airship a reality. The combination of photovoltaic and advanced energy storage systems delivers the necessary power to perform the airship functions. **Propulsion units will maintain the airship's geostationary position above the jet stream,** *propel it aloft and guide its takeoff and landing during ascent and descent. Lighter-than-air vehicles, operating at altitudes above controlled airspace under the control of a manned ground station, give users the flexibility to change payload equipment when the airship returns to its operational base to perform different tasks.*

This updated concept of a proven technology takes lighter-than-air vehicles into a realm that gives users **<u>capabilities on par with satellites at a fraction of the cost (1 to 2 orders of magnitude less)</u>.** *The HAA will also integrate reconfigurable, multi-mission payload suites.* **HAA is significantly less costly to deploy and operate than other airborne platforms, and supports critical missions for defense, homeland security, <u>and other civil applications</u>.** *Its operational persistence eliminates the need for in-theater logistic support.* **In position, an airship would survey a 600-mile diameter area and millions of cubic miles of airspace.**

Lockheed Martin, Akron, received its first production contract for a lighter-than-air vehicle in **1928.** *Since that time, Lockheed Martin has built more than* **8,000 lighter-than-air platforms.**

ILC DOVER
creating what's next »

In their *'About Us'* page, ILC Dover gives some insight into their business, demonstrating close ties with NASA:

*Known for the **production of space suits for NASA**, we leverage our vast materials, engineering, process, and design experience to create high performance systems for a wide range of industries. We provide:*

- ***Advanced Space Suits** and <u>**Space Inflatables to the space market**</u>*
- ***Airships, Aerostats and Unmanned Aerial Vehicles to the aerospace market***

Coincidentally, ILC Dover also has a key role in the *'High-Altitude Airships'* market, with a decades-long partnership with the U.S. Navy and NASA:

*ILC Dover has been involved in the **design and development of high-altitude airships since the early 1980s supporting development programs for the Navy and NASA**. The subsequent growth of the cellular phone market generated renewed interest in the use of high-altitude airships as a means of providing economical coverage in developing countries. ILC has supported Lockheed Martin in the development of HAA vehicles including HALE-D (High Altitude Long Endurance Demonstrator).*

*We are also supporting **DARPA's ISIS** (Integrated Sensor is Structure) high altitude program. Integrated Sensor Is Structure (ISIS) is a **disruptive Command and Control, Intelligence, Surveillance and Reconnaissance (C2ISR) extremely large dual-aperture radar capability integrated in a fully autonomous stratospheric unmanned airship**.*

Airship Challenge!

With their vast knowledge of 'outer space', NASA also sets their sights closer to home. In a 2014 nasa.gov article titled '*NASA Seeks Comments on Possible Airship Challenge*', NASA astrophysicist Jason Rhodes demonstrates their interest in airships:

"The 65,000-foot mark (**Stith**: roughly 12 miles above ground) *is the sweet spot where the airship would get as high as possible while still having enough air to propel against, because it needs propulsion to stay in the same spot. It's also a good altitude in terms of average wind speed," Rhodes said.*

So far, no powered airship has been able to sustain this altitude for more than eight hours. Balloons do fly at this height -- for example, weather balloons -- but they are subject to prevailing winds, and may be less reliable.

An airship **could have a telescope on either end of it to create high-resolution images of stars and other celestial objects**, *for example.*

The NASA article goes on to explain why airships are superior to 'satellites':

"You would be able to follow weather patterns, even **get above a hurricane. A satellite can't do that because its orbit can't be changed,"** *Rhodes said.*

There are also potential **commercial uses. For instance, telecommunications companies could make use of the airships to provide wireless Internet** *to remote areas.*

*"**We're only limited by our imagination**," Rhodes said.*

GPS – ~~Ground~~ Global Positioning System

A 2010 blog post on nokia.com titled *'Oh Brother, Where Art Thou?'* describes how 'satellites' are responsible for GPS:

Today we can figure out where we are by using GPS which is one of the most impressive feats of modern technology. The GPS system consists of **24-32 satellites (29 at the moment) in medium earth orbit**. *A GPS receiver basically measures the time delays (and hence the distance) between itself and any satellite it can see. This distance measurement allows the receiver to know it is on the surface of a sphere, a precise distance from any one satellite. By combining the data from* **three or more satellites**, *a precise location point can be determined, the place where all these surfaces intersect. Today GPS* **and its various modifications** *can determine location on the Earth to a precision of a few centimeters.*

Interestingly, in the same technology has been available on earth for many years, at a fraction of the cost of sending satellites to 'space'.

A 2009 article on windowscentral.com titled *'Google Maps Now Does Location by Tower Triangulation'* describes the technological feat:

The newest version of Google Maps will now take a shot at guessing your current location by looking at the relative signal strength of the **cell towers** *around you. You can watch a cutesy YouTube Video to get an idea of how it works.* **No GPS necessary, baby**!

One would assume that boats and airplanes use satellite communications to travel overseas, but that's not the case.

Hundreds, or even thousands, of boats are out in the oceans at any given time, yet boat tracking websites – such as vesselfinder.com – are only able to track boats which are close to land. Boat tracking websites show the earth as a flat plane, and not a globe.

Ping

The technology which allows objects to be tracked has been around since at-least the 1940s.

Cell phone towers permeate the land. According to statisticbrain.com, there are approximately **215,000 cell phone towers in the United States alone**, up from 900 in 1985.

These multi-purpose 'antennas', which have been around since the early 1900s, serve a variety of purposes (as described by Wikipedia):

Antennas are essential components of all equipment that uses radio. They are used in systems such as radio broadcasting, broadcast television, two-way radio, communications receivers, radar, cell phones, and satellite communications, as well as other devices such as garage door openers, wireless microphones, Bluetooth-enabled devices, wireless computer networks, baby monitors, and RFID tags on merchandise.

The towers do everything that satellites purportedly do, at a fraction of the cost.

A 2014 article on gpsworld.com titled '*eDLoran: The Next-Gen Loran*' describes how the Loran system, which utilizes ground-based towers, offers the same 'GPS' capabilities as 'satellites':

*A new enhanced differential Loran system demonstrates 5-meter accuracy not achievable by the current DLoran system, and requires **less expensive reference stations**. A prototype tested in Rotterdam's Europort area uses standard mobile telecom networks and the Internet to reduce correction data latency — a key source of error — by one to two orders of magnitude.*

'GPS' and 'satellite' technology has *coincidentally* improved at the same rate as their ground-based *alternative*.

Under the Sea

The first undersea data cable was laid in the 1850s. Since then, the technology has improved significantly and accounts for *nearly all* international data transmission.

Resting thousands of feet under the sea, these cables – also known as submarine cables – literally connect the world.

(Wikipedia Commons description: U.S. Navy Builder 2nd Class Christopher Farmer, assigned to Dive Detachment Bravo, Underwater Construction Team 2, installs steel armor around a seafloor cable during Maintenance under 100 feet of water off the coast of the Pacific Missile Range Facility Barking Sands, Hawaii, Aug. 14, 2013. The project was part of a three-stop deployment to maintain underwater cables.)

According to submarinecablemap.com, as of March 2017, there were over 360 of these undersea cables.

The cables enable the 'interconnectedness' of the 'world wide web' and all other data streams in a most efficient and high-powered manner.

We logically assume that satellites play a role in field of international data transmission, **but that is another lie.**

An opsmag.com article titled *'Retirement at Age 25? Extending Submarine Cable's Lifespan'* describes the importance of these underground cables, demonstrating that satellite communications would pale in comparison to hard-wired earth-based transmissions:

The centrality of our submarine cable system to global economics and communications cannot be understated. There is still a common public misunderstanding that satellites are the primary method of international communications, however <u>submarine fiber optic cables now carry almost 100% of the world's international Internet, voice and data communication.</u>

A mentalfloss.com article titled '*10 Facts About the Internet's Undersea Cables*' further exposes the myth that satellites, if they were real, would not be able to compete with earth-based cables:

Submarine communications cables are faster and cheaper than satellites.

There are well over a thousand satellites in orbit, we're landing probes on comets, and we're planning missions to Mars. We're living in the future! It just seems self-evident that space would be a better way to virtually "wire" the Internet than our current method of running really long cables-slash-shark-buffets along the ocean floor. *Surely satellites would be better than a technology invented before the invention of the telephone—right? As it turns out, no. (Or at least, not yet.)* Though fiber optic cables and communications satellites were both developed in the 1960s, *satellites have a two-fold problem: latency and bit loss.* Sending and receiving signals to and from space takes time. Meanwhile, researchers have *developed optical fibers that can transmit information at 99.7% the speed of light.* For an idea of what the Internet would be like without undersea cables, visit *Antarctica, the only continent without a physical connection to the net.* The continent relies on satellites, and *bandwidth is at a premium, which is no small problem when one considers the important, data-intensive climate research underway. Today, Antarctic research stations produce more data than they can transmit through space.*

Let's Get This Straight...

Launching satellites into space for communication purposes is akin to flying an airplane down the street.

Airships are extremely low risk, low cost, and offer more benefits than satellites. High Altitude Airships do everything that satellites purportedly do:

*An un-tethered, unmanned lighter-than-air vehicle that will operate above the jet stream in a **geostationary position** to deliver persistent station keeping as a **surveillance platform, telecommunications relay, or a weather observer.***

Airships have *"**capabilities on par with satellites at a fraction of the cost**,"* demonstrating the fact that satellites would be obsolete **even if they existed**.

We are told that satellite-generated images, which almost all are admitted composites, come from outer-space, instead of high-altitude airships.

We are told that space is exceedingly **hot yet cold** because there *"aren't enough molecules for sound waves to travel through,"* yet data is supposedly seamlessly transmitted millions of miles.

We are told that 'GPS' is a satellite-based system, even though the 'GPS' signal on our phones only works when we're near cell phone towers. The poorer the reception, the worse GPS performs.

We are told that airplanes are equipped with 'GPS' technology, yet Malaysian Airlines flight MH370 apparently crashed in the middle of the ocean and is seemingly gone without a trace.

Some people claim to witness satellite-flight, including the 'International Space Station', purportedly proving that satellites exist.

Airships take the shape of their envelope, and can be made to look like anything - including a 'space station'.

*(Hot-air balloon takes the shape of Abbey of Saint Gall_(**Attribution**: Böhringer Friedrich (Foto); fliegende Kathedrale der beiden Künstler Jan Kaeser St.Gallen und Martin Zimmermann St.Gallen)*

If one really wanted to go out on a limb, they could argue that **'space' and 'satellites' are being used as cover for a classified airship program,** among other things.

Occam's Razor

Occam's Razor *(Merriam-Webster Dictionary): a scientific and philosophic rule that entities should not be multiplied unnecessarily which is interpreted as requiring that the* **simplest of competing theories be preferred to the more complex** *or that explanations of unknown phenomena be sought first in terms of known quantities*

The narrative of satellites and space is compelling, but more a fantastical fictional tale than a reality-based technology.

Settle This Once and For All

*"We are more gullible and superstitious today than we were in the Middle Ages, and an example of modern credulity is the widespread belief that the Earth is round. **The average man can advance not a single reason for thinking that the Earth is round.** He merely swallows this theory because there is something about it that appeals to **the twentieth century mentality**."*- George Bernard Shaw; Everybody's Political What's What (1944)

Proving that humanity is spinning on an *"oblate-spheroid"* should be an easy task, but there is no **tangible** evidence suggesting that to be the case.

All evidence proves the earth is flat.

Drill through the Earth!

From an early age, we learn about the layers of the earth, but the 'inner earth' remains completely unknown. 'Scientists' thought they had it figured out but were shown to be grossly incorrect.

A Soviet drilling project, the Kola Superdeep Borehole, was commissioned between 1970 and 1994.

(*Kola commemorative stamp*)

The project was intended to drill approximately 9 miles beneath the earth's surface, but they only made it a little over 7.5 miles.

The core, or center of the earth, is purported to be 4,000 miles deep. The drilling only made it a third of the way through the earth's outermost layer of crust, revealing how little is known about what lies beneath.

A February 2017 article on Mother Nature Network (mnn.com) titled '*The world's deepest hole lies hidden beneath this rusty metal cap*' describes Kola's unexpected findings:

*Before the hole was drilled, geologists could only hypothesize about the composition of the Earth's crust. Needless to say, the amount of geological data produced by the project was unprecedented. Mostly, it revealed just **how little we really know about our planet**.*

*For instance, one of the most surprising findings was the absence of the transition from granite to basalt at a depth between 3 and 6 kilometers below the surface. Previously, scientists had used seismic waves to glean information about the composition of the crust. They had discovered that a discontinuity existed at this depth, which they assumed was due to a transition in rock type. But the borehole drillers found no such transition; instead they found only more granite. It turns out that the discontinuity revealed by the seismic waves was actually due to a metamorphic change in the rock, rather than a change in rock type. It was a **humbling realization for theorists**, to say the least.*

*Even more surprising, the rock had been thoroughly fractured and was **saturated with water. Free water was not supposed to exist at such depths**. Geologists now surmise that the water consists of hydrogen and oxygen atoms that were squeezed out of the surrounding rock by enormous pressure, and is retained there due to a layer of impermeable rock above.*

*Researchers also described the mud that flowed out of the hole as "**boiling**" **with hydrogen**. The discovery of such large quantities of hydrogen gas was **highly unexpected**.*

*By far the most riveting discovery from the project, however, was the detection of **microscopic plankton fossils** in rocks over 2 billion years old, found **four miles beneath the surface**. These "microfossils" represented about 24 ancient species, **and were encased in organic compounds which somehow survived the extreme pressures and temperatures that exist so far beneath the Earth**.*

*The final mystery revealed by the borehole was the reason drilling operations had to be abandoned. Once the drill reached depths in excess of about 10,000 feet, the temperature gradient suddenly began to increase unexpectedly. At the hole's maximum depth, **temperatures*** *skyrocketed to 356 degrees Fahrenheit, which was much higher than the 212 degrees Fahrenheit originally predicted. The **drill was rendered useless** at such temperatures.*

It is safe to say that drilling through the earth isn't happening anytime soon.

Instead, the elusive and secretive 'ice desert' on 'the bottom of the globe' contains many of the secrets of mankind's *real* history – **if only we were allowed to go there**...

Antarctica - The Mystery Spot

For *"environmental protection"* and 'scientific research', Antarctica is tightly regulated. In 1959 a "Treaty" was signed, essentially preventing the independent exploration of Antarctica.

"The Antarctic Treaty" has been signed by all large industrial countries, ensuring that no 'rogue' elements make their way in to *pollute the ice sheet.*

The official website of the Antarctic Treaty, ats.aq, describes the main objective of the "treaty":

*The main purpose of the Antarctic Treaty, which was signed in Washington on December 1, 1959, is to ensure "in the interest of all mankind that Antarctica **shall continue for ever** to be used exclusively for peaceful purposes and shall not become **the scene or object of international discord.** "*

The only people who travel to Antarctica are those who are there on official business; the "treaty" website continues:

*Parties implement the Antarctic Treaty and its Environmental Protocol **into the domestic law. National legislations establish a permitting regime for activities in Antarctica, and eligible visitors are <u>required to obtain the necessary permits in advance</u> from the relevant Competent Authority of each Antarctic Treaty Party.***

Composites Only

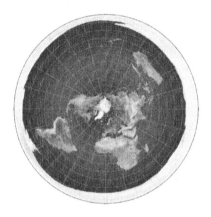

(map of flat earth encased by Antarctica)

For all of the satellites orbiting 'space', and the airships floating miles above the earth, there don't appear to be **any** *actual* photos of the **entire** 'continent' of Antarctica.

While there are purportedly photos of the entire earth from space, none provide a full image of Antarctica.

The most popular 'photo' of Antarctica is a composite of 'satellite images' provided by NASA:

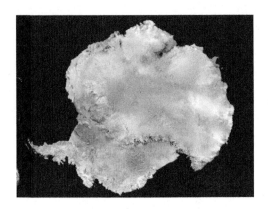

We are told that Antarctica is roughly the size of the United States and Mexico combined. At around 5.4 million miles (14 million kilometers), the 'continent' is separated from South America by only 600 miles (965 kilometers).

The following NASA composite, known as 'Earth at Night,' demonstrates the proximity between the continents and Antarctica, which appears like more of an outer-border than a typical 'continent':

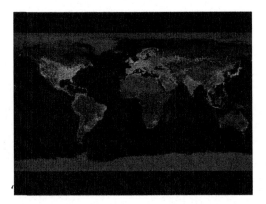

Shot Through the Heart

A trek beginning on one coast of Antarctica, following a straight line and passing through **the center**, then finishing on the opposite 'coast', would surely prove that Antarctica is indeed an island continent on the South Pole of the earth.

The following logo of the United States Antarctic Program demonstrates some of the routes (red lines) which would prove this case, **but those routes are never traversed.**

The 'journeys through Antarctica' focus on 'explorers' going to the South Pole, then turning around and heading back.

There is **no proof of the South Pole actually existing.** In documentaries and footage from the South Pole, there is no compelling geographic footage, such as compass readings, offering any evidence of a 'South Pole'.

The 'South Pole' is also said to move about 10 meters (**33** *feet*) per year, since it purportedly resides on a *"moving ice sheet."*

When explorers make their way 'across' the continent, the trips are **always** slow, difficult, and have a great back-story.

In early 2016, an 'adventurer' who attempted to *"cross Antarctica"* reportedly had to stop thirty miles from the end.

Characterizing the trip as 'crossing' Antarctica is a stretch, as the route started towards the *"South Pole"* then veered off in another direction.

Instead of utilizing a snowmobile, which would make quick work of the journey, Henry Worsley skied, consistent with most of the official Antarctic 'adventurers'.

A nytimes.com article titled *'Henry Worsley, a British Adventurer Trying to Cross Antarctica, Dies at 55'* describes the 'epic challenge':

*Attempting to be the first person to **cross Antarctica on foot**, unassisted and unsupported, he crossed more than 900 miles and **was forced**, by exhaustion and ill health, to call for help 30 miles from his journey's intended end.*

*The death was reported on the website of **the Royal Foundation, the philanthropic agency** of the Duke and Duchess of Cambridge and Prince Harry. Mr. Worsley, a career soldier before he retired from the British military in October, was making his trek to raise money for the Endeavour Fund, a **Royal Foundation project** that supports the recovery of wounded and sick service members.*

"We have lost a friend, but he will remain an inspiration to us all," Prince William, Duke of Cambridge, said in a statement.

The article continues to describe Antarctic 'achievements', like how Felicity Aston *"**skied alone across Antarctica**"*:

*An undertaking requiring **enormous physical strength and stamina**, Mr. Worsley's final journey was "**a feat of endurance never before achieved," as he described it**. (A Norwegian explorer, Borge Ousland, crossed Antarctica alone and unsupported in 1996-97, but he used a kite to pull his sled. In 2012, a British woman, Felicity Aston, **skied alone across Antarctica**, but she had two supply drops.)*

The journeys are emotional and heroic efforts, bringing mankind to the edge of death and testing the limits of the human spirit. The reality is the "continent," which is said to be essentially a large ice 'desert,' should be easily **traversed on a snowmobile in a matter of days**.

Antarctica has an average annual temperature of -58 degrees Fahrenheit (-50 Celsius), but with **no rain** – supposedly in *over 2 million years* – the 'ice desert' is easily traversed.

A 2012 article on cnn.com exposes the *emotional* dangers faced by those traveling 'across' Antarctica.

In the article, titled *'First woman to cross Antarctic solo: I've never felt so alone'*, Felicity Aston, credited with being the first woman to "cross" Antarctica solo, is profiled.

Aston skied 1,084 miles in 59 days, demonstrating the ease with which Antarctica could be 'crossed' by snowmobile or any other suitable vehicle.

An image of the route, pictured in the article, shows only a fraction of the "continent" being 'crossed', **consistent with other reported 'crossings'.**

The article describes the trials and tribulations associated with 'crossing' Antarctica:

*Despite the **endless physical dangers**, Aston says the **real challenge** is **winning the mental battle with solitude.***

"It became the biggest struggle of the whole trip," she said. *"Every single morning, the first thing that struck me was, 'Oh my goodness, I can't do this, I don't want to be here, I've made a terrible mistake.'*

*"I realized that the real (trick) of this **would not be how strong I was or how much experience I had, it would literally be getting out of that tent."***

But each day, she would get out of the tent and repeat exactly the same routine. After 40 days, she says she started noticing changes.

*"I realized **I would go a whole day and really not think about anything at all. My head was completely empty,**" she said.*

Hallucinations and strange sensations came next: "The sun became really important to me," she added.

These 'crossings' are public relations campaigns, meant to keep the 'story' moving.

Just Do It!

In 2011, Norwegian Jarle Andhøy and his crew set out to reach the 'South Pole'. They departed from New Zealand by yacht, landing in Antarctica and taking quad bikes to reach the 'South Pole'.

Due to a nasty storm in the region, the ship – and the three sailors aboard it at the time – was never seen or heard from again.

Andhøy thinks there is more to the story than what is officially reported. In *Rogue Antarctica yacht trip: 'I must have answers'* (as reported on stuff.co.nz), Andhøy describes his doubts:

*"**For me it is unreal** that a boat with three men, so much deck equipment and cargo is **lost without a trace**, except for a torn inflatable.*

"They found the only piece of equipment during the search, water bottles and various trifles.

*"But we had a **lot more on board that definitely should have come up.**"*

Reports of independent exploration of Antarctica are few and far between, **but needed** in order to make headway on the research.

Going in Circles

Sailing around the 'continent' would shed light on the true nature of Antarctica. Claims of *"circumnavigation"* of Antarctica are nothing new, but they **all** share similar characteristics.

'The Antarctica Cup Ocean Race', described on acronautic.com, claims to *"circumnavigate"* Antarctica.

The race is *"a non-stop race of over 14,000 nautical miles,"* with the racers only aware that they are "circumnavigating" the continent because that is what they are being told.

The *"360 degree Racetrack"* is equipped with state of the art technology, preventing anyone from veering off-course and accidentally 'crashing into icebergs', while offering fun prizes for the winners:

• *Introducing* **electronic 'Lanes' and 'Gates'** *to keep the racing fleet clear of dense iceberg territory.*

• *Three (3) 'Lanes', eighteen (18) 'Gates' of the course creating 18 'Sectors' for which there will be individual prizes – creating 18 'races-within-a-race'.*

Unbeknownst to the racers, they are actually just **sailing a large circle in the middle of the ocean**.

The "racetrack" doesn't actually get near Antarctica itself, but instead to the agreed-upon *nautical* border, which is in the middle of the ocean:

The Southern Ocean officially starts below latitude 60° South (International Hydrographic Organisation (IHO) www.iho.shom.fr/ . Latitude 60° South is also **the border of the Antarctic Treaty Organisation** *www.antarctica.ac.uk/aboutantarctica/treaty*

The commercial airliners buzzing overhead don't deter the racers from believing that they are circumnavigating Antarctica:

*For observation purposes, it is possible to **overfly a greater proportion of the Racetrack with flights** out of airports located on the east and west coast of Australia , New Zealand , South America , South Africa , and Antarctica .*

A true circumnavigation of Antarctica would allow ships to sail with the 'continent' in-view the entire time, starting at one end and finishing when you returned back to the beginning point... **But those types of circumnavigations don't occur around Antarctica.**

'Midnight Sun'

The North Pole region experiences sunlight for 24 hours per day, referred to as the 'midnight sun', for approximately six months out of the year.

The phenomenon is **witnessed by people** living in parts of Canada, Greenland, Iceland, Finland, Norway, Russia, Sweden, and the U.S. state of Alaska.

Antarctica is also said to experience the 'midnight sun' for a few weeks each year around Christmas, however this phenomenon is **not witnessed by any indigenous populations of people**.

Instead, time-lapse videos are offered as 'proof'.

The time-lapse videos of Antarctica, found on the U.S. Department of Commerce's website (noaa.gov), are clearly spliced and edited.

Evidence of a 'midnight sun' should be abundant and ubiquitous, yet we are expected to trust 'official' edited footage.

There is **no continuous footage** of the sun making an uninterruped circle in the sky; or with shadows of flags completing a full-circle around the flag.

If there was actual footage of the 'midnight sun' in Antarctica, it would be paraded as 'proof' that the earth is spherical.

Earth's Hidden History

*"**Who controls the past controls the future**. Who controls the present controls the past."* – George Orwell; *'1984'*

The teachings of textbooks don't match the *actual* evidence. By connecting the dots, we can begin to understand that there is more to our past than we have been led to believe.

The Great Flood

('The Deluge'; by Gustave Doré; 1865; *La Sainte Bible*)

Those who speak of 'The Great Flood' are seen as misguided 'Bible-literalists', even though ancient cultures throughout the entire world describe the event.

Mainstream science also backs the claim, yet most see 'the deluge' as a myth.

Textbooks point to gradual glacial melting causing sea levels to rise, but the evidence instead points to a massive and catastrophic 'deluge'.

Robert Ballard, credited with finding the Titanic, claims to have proof that the Biblical flood was an actual event, *"causing floods all around the world."*

In an abcnews.com article titled *'Evidence Noah's Biblical Flood Happened, Says Robert Ballard',* details of the findings are outlined:

*The story of Noah's Ark and the Great Flood is one of the most famous from the Bible, and now an acclaimed underwater archaeologist thinks he has found proof that **the biblical flood was actually based on real events.***

In an interview with Christiane Amanpour for ABC News, Robert Ballard, one of the world's best-known underwater archaeologists, talked about his findings. His team is probing the depths of the Black Sea off the coast of Turkey in search of traces of an ancient civilization hidden underwater since the time of Noah.

Ballard's team was investigating a specific area, and the findings point to **a massive and catastrophic flood which occurred rapidly**:

*According to a **controversial theory** proposed by two Columbia University scientists, there really was one in the Black Sea region. They believe that the now-salty Black Sea was once an isolated freshwater lake surrounded by farmland, until it was flooded by an **enormous wall of water** from the rising Mediterranean Sea. **The force of the water was two hundred times that of Niagara Falls, sweeping away everything in its path.***

Fascinated by the idea, Ballard and his team decided to investigate.

*"We went in there to look for the flood," he said. "**Not just a slow moving, advancing rise of sea level, but a really big flood that then stayed... The land that went under stayed under.**"*

***Four hundred feet below the surface, they unearthed an ancient shoreline**, proof to Ballard that a **catastrophic event did happen** in the Black Sea. By carbon dating shells found along the shoreline, Ballard said he believes they have established a timeline for that catastrophic event, which he estimates happened around 5,000 BC. Some experts believe this was around the time when Noah's flood could have occurred.*

The article continues to describe the parallels between what occurred in the Black Sea region and what the ancient cultures **throughout the world** have been telling us for years:

*"The earlier Mesopotamian stories are very similar **where the gods are sending a flood to wipe out humans**," said biblical archaeologist Eric Cline. "There's one man they choose to survive. He builds a boat and*

brings on animals and lands on a mountain and lives happily ever after? *I would argue that it's the same story."*

A 2016 article on businessinsider.com titled *'These skeletons prove a mythical megaflood really happened'* describes **a similar flood – at a similar time – in China.**

Thousands of years ago, **the legend goes,** *an ancient people living along the banks of the Yellow River in northern China experienced* **a flood unlike any before it.**

The article goes on to describe the *"catastrophic flood":*

On Thursday, Cohen and an interdisciplinary team of scientists **presented the first definitive evidence** *— from the victims of a killer earthquake —* **that a catastrophic flood** *really did occur along the Yellow River about 4,100 years ago,* **overwhelming communities more than 1,200 miles downstream.**

The collaboration pulled together geological evidence for floods with the archaeological remains of a prehistoric site downriver to pinpoint the severity flood and its date, which matches well with early Bronze Age China — and the story of Yu. Their findings will be published in the journal Science.

"This is the **first time a flood of scale large enough to account for it has been found,"** *Cohen said. "***The outburst flood could've caused social disruptions lasting downstream for years.***"*

Fossils

(fossils from 'millions of years ago')

Perfectly preserved fossils are ubiquitous **throughout the world**. An article on bbc.co.uk titled *'Natural selection and evolution'* describes two of the common ways fossils form:

- *Casts or impressions, such as **foot prints**, can be **covered by layers of sediments**. These eventually become rock, so preserving the casts.*
- *Hard body parts, such as bones, shells and leaves, can be **covered by layers of sediments**. Over time the parts are gradually replaced by minerals.*

Logic and reason dictate that the only way that living creatures and their foot prints could be *'flash-fossilized'* is due to **sudden and drastic flooding**.

The processes which are attributed to fossilization aren't common today. When a fish dies, it is completely gone within a matter of days, leaving no trace. An animal dies in the woods and in a few weeks, if not sooner, there is no trace..

'Science' teaches that fossils are from millions of years ago, but a **more recent timeframe** appears to be in order.

Piri Reis

(Piri Reis Map)

The Piri Reis Map demonstrates that Antarctica was once a much larger landmass.

A 2014 article on theepochtimes.com titled *'Piri Reis Map: Evidence of a Very Advanced Prehistoric Civilization?'* describes how Antarctica purportedly looked long before being *"discovered"* in 1818:

*A map created by Turkish admiral and cartographer Piri Reis in 1513 has intrigued scholars both mainstream and alternative since it was discovered in Istanbul's Topkapi Palace in 1929. On the alternative side, it's said that this map may **show Antarctica hundreds of years before the continent was discovered** (it was discovered in 1818). Furthermore, it is said to depict Antarctica as it was in a very remote age, before it was covered with ice.*

*In short, it could indicate **advanced knowledge passed down from a prehistoric sea-faring civilization. Mainstream scientists refute this hypothesis, but remain intrigued** by the mysteries this map presents.*

The article continues to describe a massive landmass which no longer exists:

*On the Piri Reis map, it seems **South America is strangely misshapen.** While Brazil is clearly discernable, as the coastline is traced further south, **it juts out east, seemingly depicting a landmass in a place where no such landmass exists today. This is the purported southern continent, also known as Terra Australis, or what some say is Antarctica.***

This information does not match what is taught in textbooks, though it appears to be 'cartographically-correct' (the article continues):

Today, more than 98 percent of the Antarctic continent is covered by glacier ice, according to Olafur Ingolfsson, a geologist at the University of Iceland.

*Captain Lorenzo W. Burroughs, a U.S. Air Force captain in the cartographic section, wrote a letter to Dr. Charles Hapgood in 1961 saying that the "Antarctica" depicted on the Piri Reis map **seems to accurately show Antarctica's coast as it is under the ice.***

***"The Princess Martha Coast of Queen Maud Land, Antarctica, appears to be truly represented on the southern sector of the Piri Reis map. The agreement of the Piri Reis map with the seismic profile of this area made by the Norweigan-British-Swedish expedition of 1949 ... places beyond a reasonable doubt the conclusion that the original source maps must have been made before the present Antarctic ice cap covered the Queen Maud Land coasts,"** Burroughs wrote, as recorded in Dr. Hapgood's 1966 book "Maps of the Ancient Sea Kings."*

A 2012 article on nasa.gov titled '*Study Finds Ancient Warming Greened Antarctica*' confirms that 'Antarctica' once boasted **a much more hospitable environment**:

A new university-led study with NASA participation finds ancient Antarctica was much warmer and wetter than previously suspected. The climate was suitable to support **substantial vegetation -- including stunted trees** -- along the edges of the frozen continent.

The team of scientists involved in the study, published online June 17 in Nature Geoscience, was led by Sarah J. Feakins of the University of Southern California in Los Angeles, and **included researchers from NASA**'s Jet Propulsion Laboratory in Pasadena, Calif., and Louisiana State University in Baton Rouge.

By examining plant leaf wax remnants in sediment core samples taken from beneath the Ross Ice Shelf, the research team found summer temperatures along the Antarctic coast **15 to 20 million years ago** were **20 degrees Fahrenheit (11 degrees Celsius) warmer than today**, with temperatures reaching as high as 45 degrees Fahrenheit (7 degrees Celsius). **Precipitation levels also were found to be several times higher than today.**

Atlantis – The Lost Empire

In 360 BC, Plato describes the 'mythical' Atlantis in his works *Timaeus* and *Critias*:

For it is related in our records how once upon a time your State stayed the course of a mighty host, which, starting from a distant point in the Atlantic ocean, was insolently advancing to attack the whole of Europe, and Asia to boot. For the ocean there was at that time navigable; for in front of the mouth which you Greeks call, as you say, 'the pillars of Heracles,' there lay an island **which was larger than Libya and Asia together;** *and it was possible for the travelers of that time to cross from it to the other islands, and from the islands to the whole of the continent over against them which encompasses that veritable ocean. For all that we have here, lying within the mouth of which we speak, is evidently a haven having a narrow entrance;* **but that yonder is a real ocean, and the land surrounding it may most rightly be called, in the fullest and truest sense, a continent. Now in this island of Atlantis there existed a confederation of kings, of great and marvelous power, which held sway over all the island, and over many other islands also and parts of the continent.**

Plato's account of the powerful civilization which was wiped out by a massive flood is discredited by 'scholars'.

An article on nationalgeographic.com titled *'Atlantis—True Story or Cautionary Tale?'* states that Plato's claims should not be taken literally:

If the writing of the ancient Greek philosopher Plato had not contained so much truth about the human condition, his name would have been forgotten centuries ago.

*But one of his most famous stories—**the cataclysmic destruction of the ancient civilization of Atlantis—is almost certainly false. So why is this story still repeated more than 2,300 years after Plato's death**?*

*"It's a story that captures the imagination," says James Romm, a professor of classics at Bard College in Annandale, New York. "**It's a great myth**. It has a lot of elements that people love to fantasize about."*

*Plato told the story of Atlantis around 360 B.C. The **founders of Atlantis, he said, were half god and half human.** They created a utopian civilization and became a great naval power. Their home was made up of concentric islands separated by wide moats and linked by a canal that penetrated to the center. The lush islands contained gold, silver, and other precious metals and supported an abundance of rare, exotic wildlife. There was a great capital city on the central island.*

*There are many theories about where Atlantis was—in the Mediterranean, off the coast of Spain, **even under what is now Antarctica.***

The article goes on to describe how no 'real' scientists think that the 'mythical' Atlantis existed:

Few, if any, scientists think Atlantis actually existed.** Ocean explorer Robert Ballard, the National Geographic explorer-in-residence who discovered the wreck of the Titanic in 1985, notes that **"no Nobel laureates" have said that what Plato wrote about Atlantis is true.

137

When anomalies are spotted in Antarctica, they are brushed off as natural formations and no debate, nor *official* exploration, ensues.

The following ~~airship~~ satellite image of Antarctica show what appears to be pyramidal, however we are told that that is certainly not the case.

A November 2016 article on cbsnews.com titled '*New pyramid in Antarctica? Not quite, say geologists*' describes – using only logic and reason, and **no evidence** - how the pyramid-looking structure is certainly not a pyramid:

*An Antarctic mountain with a **unique, pyramid-like shape** is suddenly internet-famous, with countless theorists contemplating its origin. Some are wondering whether an ancient civilization created the rocky, pyramidal structure, and others are pointing toward outer space, speculating about the involvement of aliens.*

*But **Occam's razor** — the idea that the simplest explanation is usually the right one — points to a far more mundane cause: **Those steep, pyramid-like sides are likely the work of hundreds of millions of years of erosion**, experts told Live Science.*

*"**This is just a mountain that looks like a pyramid**," Eric Rignot, a professor of Earth system science at the University of California, Irvine, told Live Science in an email. "**Pyramid shapes are not impossible —***

138

many peaks partially look like pyramids, but they only have one to two faces like that, rarely four."

The dots are not connected in textbooks or by mainstream 'scientists'.

Riaan Booysen, of riaanbooysen.com, describes himself as *"a practicing engineer that holds a PhD degree in Electromagnetics and have been awarded Senior Membership of the IEEE."*

In an article titled *'Terra Australis Incognita - Atlantis'*, Booysen describes what the historical record *truly* tells us:

*It is argued that Terra Australis Incognita, the **'imaginary' southern continent which appears on virtually all early maps of the world, was a real continent that matches Plato's mythical Atlantis in many respects.** Maps showing three different forms of Terra Australis suggest a continent of which the central plain was gradually being flooded before it ultimately disappeared under the water. The submarine topography of New Zealand closely matches one of these maps and ancient legends of South America suggest that disappearance of the continent was caused by the impact of a comet. **It is argued that Antarctica must have been ice free up to 12,000 years ago**, when the impact of a comet caused a tsunami which **nearly caused the extinction of mankind**, the tsunami having been recorded in the **Bible as the Great Flood**.*

Description of Atlantis, <u>the sunken continent</u>

*Plato, in his dialogues Timaeus and Critias[1], relates the legend of a powerful nation that around 9500 BCE inhabited a continent greater in size than ancient Libya and Asia combined. This nation attacked and conquered Europe and Asia, with only the Greeks being able to prevail against them. **Sometime after the invasion, however, the Greeks and the Atlanteans were 'swallowed up' by the sea in a single grievous day and night.***

*The continent, which lay beyond the Pillars of Hercules, is described as having had a central, **"rectangular and oblong" shaped plain with a 3:2 length-to-width ratio, surrounded by mountains but with an opening***

139

to the sea. *A mountain that was "low on all sides" ran through the centre of the plain.* **Atlantis had ten states or provinces, each with its own king and capital city. The fabulous royal city of Atlantis was surrounded by circles of sea over which bridges had been built. The royal city of Atlantis alone had a standing army of what based on calculations must have been close to 1 million soldiers and a fleet of 1200 warships**[2]. *The capital cities of the other states had armies of varying sizes, with a total population of between 64 and 100 million people*[3].

It is no wonder that those in power intend for Antarctica to be off-limits **"for ever."**

It Was Written

Virtually all writings from ancient times describe a flat and *'immovable'* earth.

Robert Schadewald, former President of the National Center for Science Education, studied flat-earth literature and philosophy, writing extensively on the subject.

Schadewald was a noted opponent of 'Creationism', and fought to keep that and other 'pseudoscience' out of schools.

In a 1987 article titled *'The Flat earth Bible,'* (originally published in *The Bulletin of the Tychonian Society)*, Shadewald demonstrates how the flat-earth concept was previously based solely on the written word:

*When I first became interested in the flat earthers in the early 1970s, I was surprised to learn that flat earthism in the English-speaking world **is and always has been entirely based upon the Bible**.*

While much of the current flat-earth research is based on testable science and deductive reasoning, the **written-word case is compelling – no matter one's religious affiliation**. Schadewald continues:

*Except among Biblical inerrantists, **it is generally agreed that the Bible describes an immovable earth**. At the 1984 National Bible-Science Conference in Cleveland, geocentrist James N. Hanson told me **there are hundreds of scriptures that suggest the earth is immovable**. I suspect some must be a bit vague, but here are a few obvious texts:*

1 Chronicles 16:30: "He has fixed the earth firm, immovable."

Psalm 93:1: "Thou hast fixed the earth immovable and firm ..."

Psalm 96:10: "He has fixed the earth firm, immovable ..."

Psalm 104:5: "Thou didst fix the earth on its foundation so that it never can be shaken."

Isaiah 45:18: "...who made the earth and fashioned it, and himself fixed it fast..."

Scriptural quotes, unless otherwise noted, are from the New English Bible. Hebrew and Greek translations are from Strong's Exhaustive Concordance of the Bible. The Biblical cosmology is never explicitly stated, so it must be pieced together from scattered passages. The Bible is a composite work, so there is no a priori reason why the cosmology assumed by its various writers should be relatively consistent, but it is. **The Bible is, from Genesis to Revelation, a flat earth book.**

This is hardly surprising. As neighbors, the ancient Hebrews had the Egyptians to the southwest and the Babylonians to the northeast. Both civilizations had flat earth cosmologies. **The Biblical cosmology closely parallels the Sumero-Babylonian cosmology, and it may also draw upon Egyptian cosmology.**

*The Babylonian universe was shaped like a **modern domed stadium**. The Babylonians considered the earth essentially flat, with a **continental mass surrounded by ocean**. The vault of the sky was a physical object resting upon the ocean's waters** (and perhaps also upon pillars). Sweet (salt-free) waters below the Earth sometimes manifest themselves as springs.* **The Egyptian universe was also enclosed, but it was rectangular instead of round.** *Indeed, it was shaped much like an old-fashioned steamer trunk. (**The Egyptians pictured the goddess Nut stretched across the sky as the enclosing dome.***) What was the Hebrew view of the universe?*

The Order of Creation

The Genesis creation story provides the first key to the Hebrew cosmology. **The order of creation makes no sense from a conventional perspective but is perfectly logical from a flat earth viewpoint.** *The earth was created on the first day, and it was "without form and void (Genesis 1:2)." On the second day, a vault the "firmament" of the King James version was created to divide the waters, some being above and some below the vault. Only on the fourth day were the sun, moon, and stars created, and they were placed "in" (not "above") the vault.*

142

The Vault of Heaven

*The vault of heaven is a crucial concept. The word "**firmament**" appears
in the King James version of the Old Testament **17 times**, and in each
case it is translated from the Hebrew word raqiya, which meant the
visible vault of the sky. The word raqiya comes from riqqua, meaning
"**beaten out**." In ancient times, brass objects were either cast in the form
required or beaten into shape on an anvil. A good craftsman could beat
a lump of cast brass into a thin bowl. Thus, Elihu asks Job, "Can you beat
out [raqa] the vault of the skies, as he does, hard as a mirror of cast
metal (Job 37:18)?"*

*Elihu's question shows that the **Hebrews considered the vault of heaven
a solid, physical object**. Such a large dome would be a tremendous feat
of engineering. The Hebrews (and supposedly Yahweh Himself)
considered it exactly that, and this point is hammered home by five
scriptures:*

Job 9:8, "...who by himself spread out the heavens [shamayim]..."

*Psalm 19:1, "The heavens [shamayim] tell out the glory of God, the vault
of heaven [raqiya] reveals his handiwork."*

Psalm 102:25, "...the heavens [shamayim] were thy handiwork."

*Isaiah 45:12, "I, with my own hands, stretched out the heavens
[shamayim] and caused all their host to shine..."*

*Isaiah 48:13, "...with my right hand I formed the expanse of the sky
[shamayim]..."*

*If these verses are about a mere illusion of a vault, they are surely
much ado about nothing. Shamayim comes from shameh, a root
meaning to be lofty. It literally means the sky. Other passages complete
the picture of the **sky as a lofty, physical dome**. God "sits throned on the
vaulted roof of earth [chuwg], whose inhabitants are like grasshoppers.
He stretches out the skies [shamayim] like a curtain, he spreads them
out like a tent to live in...[Isaiah 40:22]." Chuwg literally means "circle"
or "encompassed." By extension, it can mean roundness, **as in a
rounded dome or vault**. Job 22:14 says God "walks to and fro on the
vault of heaven [chuwg]." In both verses, the use of chuwg **implies a***

physical object, on which one can sit and walk. *Likewise, the context in both cases requires elevation. In Isaiah, the elevation causes the people below to look small as grasshoppers. In Job, God's eyes must penetrate the clouds to view the doings of humans below. Elevation is also implied by Job 22:12: "Surely God is at the zenith of the heavens [shamayim] and looks down on all the stars, high as they are."*

This picture of the cosmos is reinforced by Ezekiel's vision. The Hebrew word raqiya appears five times in Ezekiel, four times in Ezekiel 1:22-26 and once in Ezekiel 10:1. **In each case the context requires a literal vault or dome.** *The vault appears above the "living creatures" and glitters* **"like a sheet of ice."** *Above the vault is a throne of sapphire (or lapis lazuli). Seated on the throne is "a form in human likeness," which is radiant and "like the appearance of the glory of the Lord." In short, Ezekiel saw a vision of God sitting throned on the vault of heaven, as described in Isaiah 40:22.*

The Shape of the Earth

Disregarding the dome, the **essential flatness of the earth's surface is required** *by verses like Daniel 4:10-11. In Daniel, the king "saw a tree of great height at the centre of the earth...reaching with its top to the sky and visible to the earth's farthest bounds." If the earth were flat, a sufficiently tall tree would be visible to "the earth's farthest bounds," but this is impossible on a spherical earth. Likewise, in describing the temptation of Jesus by Satan, Matthew 4:8 says, "Once again, the devil took him to a very high mountain, and showed him all the kingdoms of the world [cosmos] in their glory." Obviously, this would be possible only if the earth were flat. The same is true of Revelation 1:7: "Behold, he is coming with the clouds! Every eye shall see him..."*

144

Book of Enoch

Schadewald continues to describe the Book of Enoch, which many consider to be the most compelling ancient 'flat-earth' text:

The most important ancient document describing Hebrew cosmology is 1 Enoch (sometimes called the Ethiopic Book of Enoch), one of those long, disjointed, scissors and paste jobs beloved by ancient scribes. For a dozen or so centuries, European scholars knew 1 Enoch only from numerous passages preserved in the patristic literature. In 1773, the Scottish adventurer James Bruce found complete copies in Ethiopia.

Numerous manuscripts of 1 Enoch have since been found in Ethiopian monasteries. Turn of the century scholars concluded that parts of the book are pre-Maccabean, and most (perhaps all) of it was composed by 100 B.C. [Charles, 1913]. These conclusions were largely vindicated when numerous fragments of 1 Enoch were found among the so-called Dead Sea Scrolls at Qumran. There have been two major English translations of 1 Enoch, the 1913 translation of R. H. Charles and the 1983 translation by E. Isaac. All of the quotations that follow come from the newer translation.

The importance of 1 Enoch is poorly appreciated outside the scholarly community. Comparison of its text with New Testament books reveals that many Enochian doctrines were taken over by early Christians. E. Isaac writes:

There is little doubt that 1 Enoch was influential in molding New Testament doctrines concerning the nature of the Messiah, the Son of Man, the messianic kingdom, demonology, the future, resurrection, final judgment, the whole eschatological theater, and symbolism. No wonder, therefore, that the book was highly regarded by many of the apostolic and Church Fathers [1986, 10].

First Enoch influenced Matthew, Luke, John, Acts, Romans, and several

145

other New Testament books. The punishment of the fallen angels described in 2 Peter seems to come directly from 1 Enoch, as does much of the imagery (or even wording) in Revelation. The Epistle of Jude contains the most dramatic evidence of its influence when it castigates "enemies of religion" as follows:

It was to them that Enoch, the seventh in descent from Adam, directed his prophecy when he said: "I saw the Lord come with his myriads of angels, to bring all men to judgment and to convict all the godless of all the godless deeds they had committed, and of all the defiant words which godless sinners had spoken against him (Jude 14- 15)."

The inner quote, 1 Enoch 1:9, is found in the original Hebrew on a recently-published Qumran fragment [Shanks, 1987, 18]. By attributing prophecy to Enoch, Jude confers inspired status upon the book.

First Enoch is important for another reason. Unlike the canonical books of the Bible, which (in my view) were never meant to teach science, **sections of 1 Enoch were intended to describe the natural world. The narrator sometimes sounds like a 2nd century B.C. Carl Sagan explaining the heavens and earth to the admiring masses. The Enochian cosmology is precisely the flat earth cosmology previously derived from the canonical books.**

The Ends of the Earth

The angel Uriel guided Enoch in most of his travels. They made several trips to **the ends of the earth, where the dome of heaven came down to the surface.** For instance, Enoch says:

I went to the extreme ends of the earth and saw there huge beasts, each different from the other and different birds (also) differing from one another in appearance, beauty, and voice. And to the east of those beasts, I saw the ultimate ends of the earth which rests on the heaven. And the gates of heaven were open, and I saw **how the stars of heaven come out**...(1 Enoch 33:1-2).

(The sharp-eyed reader will note what I suspect is an editing error in the Isaac translation. The earth resting on the heaven makes no sense. R. H.

146

Charles has "whereon the heaven rests.")

Again, Enoch says, "I went in the direction of the north, to the extreme ends of the earth, and there at the extreme end of the whole world I saw a great and glorious seat. There (also) I saw three open gates of heaven; **when it blows cold, hail, frost, snow, dew, and rain, through each one of the (gates) the winds proceed in the northwesterly direction (1** Enoch 34:1-2)." This accords well with Jeremiah 51:16 which says, "he brings up the mist from the ends of the earth, **he opens rifts for the rain** and brings the wind out of his storehouses." In subsequent chapters, Enoch journeys **"to the extreme ends of the earth"** in the west, south, and east. In each place he saw three more "open gates of heaven."

There were other things to be seen at the ends of the earth. Earlier, we deferred discussion of the King James version of Job 26:7, "He stretcheth out the north over the empty place, and hangeth the earth upon nothing." On several occasions when Enoch and the angel are **out beyond the dome of heaven, Enoch comments that there is nothing above or below.** For instance, "And I came to an empty place. And I saw (there) **neither a heaven above nor an earth below, but a chaotic and terrible place (1 Enoch 21:1-2)."** Could this be the kind of nothingness referred to in Job?

An angel also showed Enoch the storerooms of the winds (18:1) and the cornerstone of the earth (18:2).

Conspiracies Don't Exist

*"Today no war has been declared — and however fierce the struggle may be, **it may never be declared in the traditional fashion. Our way of life is under attack... We are opposed around the world by a monolithic and ruthless conspiracy that relies primarily on covert means for expanding its sphere of influence** — on infiltration instead of invasion, on subversion instead of elections, on intimidation instead of free choice, on guerrillas by night instead of armies by day. It is a system which has conscripted vast human and material resources into the building of a **tightly knit, highly efficient machine that combines military, diplomatic, intelligence, economic, scientific and political operations.** – John F. Kennedy; 1961*

Influential people, most of which would not fall into the 'conspiracy theory' camp, have warned of a well-organized and ubiquitous group seeking to surreptitiously control humanity.

While it's unclear whether these groups were initially formed to benefit mankind, it would appear that any altruistic motives are a thing of the past.

In 1956, FBI Director J. Edgar Hoover describes them as *"human creatures"*:

*The individual is handicapped by coming face to face with a **conspiracy so monstrous** he cannot believe it exists. The American mind simply has not come to a realization of the evil which has been introduced into our midst. It rejects even the assumption that **human creatures could espouse a philosophy** which must ultimately destroy all that is good and decent.*

These secretive groups, which have an affinity for ancient Egyptian symbolism, go by various names and hold significant influence over many groups. The most recognizable of these secret societies is Freemasonry, though all of these 'secret' organizations appear to operate with the same modus operandi and in the same hierarchical manner.

The Bavarian Illuminati was a secret society founded on May 1, 1776. The founder of the society, Adam Weishaupt, describes how these networks use Freemasonry as the public face while much of the activities take place 'outside the lodge':

The Great strength of our order lies in its concealment let it never appear in any place in its own name, but by another name, and another activity. None is fitter than Freemasonry. The public is accustomed to it, expect little from it, and therefore takes little notice of it.

A 2013 article on cbsnews.com titled *'Inside the secret world of the Freemasons'* provides a brief overview of the 'official' version of Freemasonry:

So what is Freemasonry? Simply put, it's the world's oldest and largest fraternity. Its membership is a Who's Who of world history -- George Washington, Benjamin Franklin, Winston Churchill, Mozart, Davy Crockett, Franklin Roosevelt, Harry Houdini, Gerald Ford, Henry Ford, John Wayne, even Colonel Sanders.

Interestingly, NASA artifacts seem to hold significance within its ranks:

Inside, the temple lodge room is a stunner. And downstairs, you can see the flag that Buzz Aldrin took to the Moon with him.

The article describes Freemasonry as nothing more than a social-club with some perks:

"When a candidate comes in through the door, he's blindfolded

*because, symbolically, he is in a state of darkness," said Vaughan, "because Masonry is all about **moving from darkness into Masonic light**."*

*As for what happens after that . . . well, **that's a secret**. But for members, Freemasonry is about **something much simpler**.*

"I have met a group of men that I enjoy being with," said Morris. "These are people that I go out to dinner with, we socialize together. They're guys I like to hang with. They're my friends."

With a long and storied history, much of which has been kept secret, belies an *organization* which has a veiled yet prominent role in world affairs.

A 2015 article on washingtontimes.com titled 'Masonic rituals live on' describes how powerful people, while not official members of these groups, are associated with their practices:

President-elect Barack Obama's swearing-in Tuesday will incorporate several elements out of America's Masonic past.

One-third of the signers of the Constitution, many of the Bill of Rights signers and America's first few presidents (except for Thomas Jefferson) were Freemasons, a fraternal organization that became public in early 18th-century England.

*Although it became fabulously popular in America, at one time encompassing 10 percent of the population, Pope Clement XII condemned Freemasonry in 1738 as heretical. The latest pronouncement was issued in 1983 by then-Cardinal Joseph Ratzinger - now Pope Benedict XVI - **who called Masonic practices "irreconcilable" with Catholic doctrine.***

*Still, as the first president, George Washington had to come up with appropriate rituals for the new country. **He borrowed many of them***

150

from Masonic rites he knew as "worshipful leader" of a lodge in Alexandria.

(image of George Washington in freemasonic attire; image not affiliated with the article)

His Masonic gavel is on display at the Capitol Visitor Center. Until this inauguration, **Washington's Masonic Bible - on which he swore his obligations as a Freemason - was used for the presidential oath of office.** President-elect Barack Obama will use Abraham Lincoln's Bible.

The worshipful master administered the Masonic oaths. This was adapted to the president vowing to serve his country in an oath administered by the top justice of the Supreme Court.

The Anti-Masonic Era

The 6th President of the United States, John Quincy Adams, was nicknamed *"the hell-hound of abolition"* due to his vehement anti-slavery stance. *Coincidentally*, Adams was also a staunch opponent of Freemasonry.

(John Quincy Adams)

In his 1833 book 'Letters on Freemasonry', President Adams denounces 'the craft':

*I do conscientiously and sincerely believe that the Order of Freemasonry, if not the greatest, is one of the **greatest moral and political evils** under which the Union is now laboring ... **a conspiracy of the few against the equal rights of the many ... Masonry ought forever to be abolished. It is wrong – essentially wrong – a seed of evil, which can never produce any good**.*

President Adams played a key role in a movement which sought to abolish Freemasonry.

The Anti-Masonic Party, which was the first official 'third-party' in the United States, was founded in 1828 and played a significant role at one time, but is now largely forgotten.

(*Anti-Masonic era publication*)

Sworn to Secrecy

Those who join secret societies and progress through the ranks are required to perform rituals and take oaths to affirm their commitment.

Charles Grandison Finney was a college president, an influential lawyer, and a theologian. Coined "the father of modern revivalism," Finney was a vocal opponent of Freemasonry and their associated rituals.

In a June 18, 1868 article in The Independent of New York titled *'Freemasons Sworn to Commit Unlawful Deeds'* (archived at gospeltruth.net), Finney describes the oath taken by members of these societies:

*In this article I can only notice a few points in the oaths of Masons; and I recommend all persons to **obtain the books in which their oaths, ceremonies, and secrets are fully revealed**. The first of their oaths is that of the Entered Apprentice. These oaths are administered in the following manner: The candidate stands on his knees, with his hands on the Holy Bible. The Worshipful Master pronounces the oath in short sentences, and the candidate repeats after him. The oath of the Entered Apprentice is as follows: "I, A.B., of my own free will and accord, in presence of Almighty God and this worshipful lodge of Free and Accepted Masons, dedicated to God and held forth to the holy order of St. John, do hereby and hereon most sincerely promise and swear that I*

154

will always hail, ever conceal, and never reveal any part or parts, art or arts, point or points of the secrets, arts, and mysteries of ancient Freemasonry, which I have received, am about to receive, or may hereafter be instructed in, to any person or persons in the known world, **except it be a true and lawful brother Mason, or within the body of a just and lawfully constituted lodge of such; and not unto him or unto them whom I shall hear so to be, but unto him and them only whom I shall find so to be after strict trial and due examination,** *or lawful information.*

*"Furthermore do **I promise and swear** that I will not write, print, stamp, stain, hew, cut, carve, indent, paint, or engrave it on anything movable or immovable under the whole canopy of Heaven, whereby or whereon the least letter, figure, character, mark, stain, shadow, or resemblance may become legible or intelligible to myself or to any other person in the known world, whereby the secrets of Masonry may be unlawfully obtained through my unworthiness.* **To all of which I do most solemnly and sincerely promise and swear, without the least equivocation, mental reservation, or self evasion of mind in me whatever; binding myself under no less penalty than to have my throat cut across, my tongue torn out by the roots, and my body buried in the rough sands of the sea at low-water mark, where the tide ebbs and flows twice in twenty-four hours.** *So help me God, and keep me steadfast in the due performance of the same."*

Skull and Bones

(*Skull and Bones logo*)

Yale secret society Skull and Bones , which was founded in 1832, is known for their *prestigious* alumni, as well as their highly strange practices. In 2001, secret video footage exposed a portion of what occurs behind closed doors.

An article on observer.com titled '*At Skull and Bones, Bush's Secret Club Initiates Ream Gore*', describes some of these rituals:

It's the primal scene of American power, of Bush family values. For two centuries, the initiation rite of Skull and Bones has shaped the character of the men who have shaped the American character, including two Presidents named Bush.

And last Saturday, April 14–for the first time ever–that long-secret rite was witnessed by a team of outsiders, including this writer.

*Using high-tech night-vision video equipment able to peer through the gloom into the inner courtyard of the Skull and Bones "**Tomb**" in New Haven, The Observer team witnessed:*

· The George W. effect: intoxicated by renewed proximity to Presidential power, a robed Bonesman posing as George W. harangued initiates in

an eerily accurate Texas drawl: "I'm gonna ream you like I reamed Al Gore" and "I'm gonna kill you like I killed Al Gore."

· Privileged Skull and Bones members mocked the assault on Abner Louima by crying out repeatedly, "Take that plunger out of my ass!"

· Skull and Bones members **hurled obscene sexual insults ("lick my bumhole")** at initiates as they were forced to kneel and **kiss a skull at the feet of the initiators.**

· Other members acted out the tableau of a **throat-cutting ritual murder.**

It's important to remember this is not some fraternity initiation. **It is an initiation far more secret—and far more significant, in terms of real power in the United States—than that of the Cosa Nostra.** If the Bushes are "the WASP Corleones"—as the ever more stingingly waspish Maureen Dowd has suggested—this is how their "made men" (and women) are made.* **It's an initiation ceremony that has bonded diplomats, media moguls, bankers and spies into a lifelong, multi-generational fellowship far more influential than any fraternity. It was—and still remains—the heart of the heart of the American establishment.**

The 2004 U.S. Presidential elections pitted two Skull and 'Bonesmen' against each other. Tim Russert of NBC's Meet the Press interviewed both John Kerry and George W. Bush, prior to Bush becoming President.

In April 2004 on 'Meet the Press', Russert asks John Kerry an awkward question:

Russert: *You both were members of Skull and Bones, the secret society at Yale. What does that tell us?*

Kerry: *Not much cause it's a secret (laughing).*

Russert: *Is there a secret handshake; a secret code?*

Kerry: *I wish there were something secret I could manifest.*

157

Russert: *322; a secret number?*

Kerry changes the subject and it is not broached again:

Kerry: *There are all kinds of secrets Tim, but one thing is not a secret: I disagree with this President's direction...*

A few months prior, on February 8, 2004, Russert interviewed George W. Bush on the program, briefly questioning his secretive background:

Russert: *You were both in Skull and Bones, the secret society...*

Bush: *It's so secret we can't talk about it.*

Russert: *What does that mean for America? The conspiracy theorists are going to go wild.*

Bush: *I'm sure they are. I don't know. I haven't seen web pages (??) yet. (Laughing)*

Russert: *Number 322?*

Earlier in the interview, President Bush describes his *philosophy*, largely influenced by 'the craft':

I'm a war president. I make decisions here in the Oval Office in foreign-policy matters with war on my mind. Again, I wish it wasn't true, but it is true. And the American people need to know they got a president who sees the world the way it is. And I see dangers that exist, and it's important for us to deal with them.

Led Astray

(*Albert Pike*)

Albert Pike was a former Grand Commander in the Scottish Rite of Freemasonry. An article on freemason.org titled '*Albert Pike and Freemasonry*' describes Pike's importance:

*Many of Pike's intimate Masonic associates called him "The Patriarch," and they said that he became "**the most eminent and best loved Mason in the World**, not merely by virtue of the exalted position which he held, but because of his high character and lovable nature, his scholarly attainments, **his writings and treatises on the law and symbolism of Masonry**, and the extraordinary fund of knowledge which he possessed on every subject, in and out of the order."*

In his 1872 book '*Morals and Dogma of the Ancient and Accepted Scottish Rite of Freemasonry*', Pike explains how the initiates within Freemasonry and **many other institutions** are being misled:

Masonry, like all the Religions, all the Mysteries, Hermeticism and Alchemy**, conceals its secrets from all except the Adepts and Sages, or the Elect, and uses **false explanations and misinterpretations of its symbols to mislead those who deserve only to be misled; to conceal the Truth,** which it calls Light from them and **to draw them away from

159

it.

High-ranking Freemason and prolific writer Manly P. Hall also exposed how low-level initiates were being deceived. In his 1923 book *'The Lost Keys of Freemasonry'*, Hall exposes the deception:

*The initiated brother realizes that his **so-called symbols and rituals are merely blinds,** fabricated by the wise to **perpetuate ideas incomprehensible to the average individual**. He also realizes that **few Masons** of today know or appreciate the mystic meaning **concealed within these rituals.***

Minions

The Cambridge Dictionary defines a *minion* as "*a person who is **not important** and who has to do what another person of higher rank **orders them to do.**"*

Unsurprisingly, many of the astronauts who claim to have set foot on the moon are/were Freemasons.

Buzz Aldrin, John Glenn, and Edgar Mitchell hold the distinction, among others.

The website for the Grand Lodge of British Columbia and Yukon, freemasonry.by.ca, proudly proclaims their affiliations in an article titled '*Freemasons in Space*':

*Freemasons have always been in the forefront of the scientific community; from the **founding of the British Royal Society** to **today's NASA programme in the United States***.

The article demonstrates how even those not actively involved in

161

Freemasonry may have ties to the group:

Neil Armstrong, Jr. is not a freemason; his father, Neil Armstrong, Sr. is an active freemason. (Ohio Grand Lodge of Freemasons records).

Fake ~~News~~ Reality

"You don't have any other society where the educated classes are so effectively indoctrinated and controlled by a subtle propaganda system – a private system including media, intellectual opinion forming magazines and the participation of the most highly educated sections of the population. Such people ought to be referred to as **"Commissars"** – for that is what their essential function is – to set up and maintain a system of doctrines and beliefs which will **undermine independent thought** and prevent a proper understanding and analysis of national and global institutions, issues, and policies."* – Noam Chomsky

We naively assume that mankind is highly-intelligent, but instead the methods used to indoctrinate and control the population have never been so clearly understood.

The current state of society was predicted **and designed** many years ago.

Aldous Huxley described many of these systems, because he was *aware of their existence.*

The Huxley family was part of British aristocracy, keenly interested in

163

and control systems.

Aldous' brother Julian was the **first** director of UNESCO (**United Nations** Educational, Scientific, and Cultural Organization), also serving as the president of the British Eugenics Society from 1959-1962.

Aldous' grandfather, Thomas Henry Huxley, was also a noted eugenicist, using his influence to advocate for Charles Darwin's theory of evolution. Thomas Henry Huxley came to be known as "Darwin's Bulldog" for his persistent advocacy of *the theory*.

In his **1932** book *'Brave New World'*, Aldous Huxley illustrates the dystopian nightmare which was being constructed for humanity; a world of mental conditioning and moral degradation, where life was predetermined and everyone knew their 'place'.

In his later years, Huxley reflected on his original novel, and how much of what he had 'predicted' had come to pass. In his 1958 book 'Brave New World Revisited', Huxley describes the state of the world, and where it was heading:

In their propaganda today's dictators rely for the most part on repetition, suppression and rationalization - the repetition of catchwords which they wish to be accepted as true, the suppression of facts which they wish to be ignored, the arousal and rationalization of passions which may be used in the interests of the Party or the State. *As the art and science of manipulation come to be better understood, the dictators of the future will doubtless learn to combine these techniques with the non-stop distractions which, in the West, are now threatening to drown in a sea of irrelevance the rational propaganda essential to the maintenance of individual liberty and the survival of democratic institutions.*

High-tech gadgets and constant distractions flood our minds, while pharmaceuticals re-wire our brain.

Huxley 'predicted' 'the pharmacological revolution':

*There will be, in the next generation or so, **a pharmacological method of making people love their servitude, and producing dictatorship without tears, so to speak, producing a kind of painless concentration camp for entire societies,** so that people will in fact have their liberties taken away from them, but will rather enjoy it, because they will be distracted from any desire to rebel by propaganda or brainwashing, or brainwashing enhanced by pharmacological methods. **And this seems to be the final revolution.***

The Bamboozle

*"If we've been bamboozled long enough, we tend to **reject any evidence of the bamboozle**. **We're no longer interested in finding out the truth.** The bamboozle has captured us. It's simply too painful to acknowledge, even to ourselves, that we've been taken. Once you give a charlatan power over you, **you almost never get it back.**" –* Carl Sagan

We have been conditioned to think a certain way, and information which goes against that programming is met with derision.

Noted author and thinker Frantz Fanon describes how *cognitive dissonance* permeates society:

*Sometimes people hold a very core belief that is very strong. When they are presented with evidence that works against that belief, the **new evidence cannot be accepted**. It would create a feeling that is extremely uncomfortable, called cognitive dissonance. And because it is so important to protect that **core belief**, they will rationalize, ignore, and even deny anything that doesn't fit with the core belief.*

Humanity is in a collective state of 'bamboozlement', content to go along with the deception.

There's No Place Like Space!

The concept of 'space' is seldom questioned. So ingrained in our minds, we cannot fathom that it is an *elaborate hoax*.

From an early age, globes populate science classes and program the ball-earth model into our young minds. Children are taught about space and planets ad nauseam before they are able to think for themselves.

'Popular' children's shows and movies about 'space' are ubiquitous:

As we get older, 'space' continues to penetrate our psyche, leaving us no doubt that it's 'real'.

Space – Be Afraid

*"The human race is a monotonous affair. Most people spend the greatest part of their time working in order to live, and what **little freedom remains so fills them with fear** that they seek out any and every means to be rid of it."* – Johann Wolfgang von Goethe; 1749-1832

With all the earth-like planets potentially harboring life, and all the dangers that come from 'space', **we have plenty to worry about**.

Asteroids!

We should never get too comfortable, because the looming threat of an asteroid or meteorite is never too far off.

Articles such as '*Earth woefully unprepared for surprise comet or asteroid, Nasa scientist warns'*, from the guardian.com, remind us that disaster is always a possibility.

Predictably, NASA offers the best chance of preventing such a cataclysm:

Scientist recommended Nasa build an interceptor rocket, with periodic testing, alongside an observer spacecraft to stop catastrophic fireballs from hitting us.

Space War!

With advanced technology in the hands of 'loose cannons', the threat of a real-life 'Space War' also looms on the horizon.

The dailystar.co.uk article titled *'Russia, USA and China are prepping for all-out SPACE WAR'* describes the repercussions of such a catastrophic event:

SUPERPOWERS are preparing to dominate in a devastating space war, **which could destroy life on Earth as we know it, experts have warned.**

As countries seek to maintain control in outer-space, competition between nations will give rise to apocalyptic cosmic attacks, according to security officials.

Nightmare scenarios might leave vast swathes of the planet in the dark as intergalactic weapons knock out satellites and launch cyber attacks.

General John Hyten, head of US Strategic Command, told CNN: "As **humans go out there, there has always been conflict.** *Conflict in the Wild West as we move in the West ... conflict twice in Europe for its horrible world wars.*

It seems that it's only a matter of time before we destroy each other, but not if the 'aliens' destroy us first!!!

Space Invaders!

"Perhaps we need some outside universal threat to make us recognize this common bond. I occasionally think how quickly our differences worldwide would vanish if we were facing an alien threat from outside this world." – Ronald Reagan (1987 speech to the United Nations)

The possibility of aliens invading and taking over earth is also a common theme in the 'sci-fi' realm.

Humanity is woefully unprepared for an 'alien invasion', we are told.

A 2013 huffingtonpost.com article titled *'Could Earth Defend Itself From An ET Invasion?'* describes a *terrifying* scenario:

*While it's true that Russia has a very sophisticated air defense system capable of engaging and taking down targets at near-space altitudes — as reported by RIA Novosti, Russia's leading news agency — there's one potential enemy that country **isn't ready to confront: aliens from space.***

During a recent conference at the Titov Main Test and Space Systems Control Center near Moscow, a journalist asked if Russia's vast array of security systems could protect the country from a possible extraterrestrial invasion, according to Russia Today.

"So far, we are not capable of that," center deputy chief Sergey Berezhnoy responded. *"**We are unfortunately not ready to fight extraterrestrial civilizations**. Our center was not tasked with it. There are too many problems on Earth and near it."*

While most people are consciously aware that an 'alien invasion' is not a real possibility, the subconscious mind is another story.

"Until you make the unconscious conscious, it will control your life and you will call it fate." – Sigmund Freud

The technology for faking apparent physical manifestations already exists.

In January 2017, express.co.uk reports on an apparent hologram of a *floating city* hovering over the Chinese city of Yueyang.

The article, titled *'Was this 'floating city' that appeared over China a glimpse into 'another dimension'?'* describes what occurred:

*A FLOATING city seen in the skies of China by **thousands of people** has sparked claims of another dimension appearing above Earth, **with aliens "highly interested" in humans**.*

*The **apparition** was allegedly seen by thousands of people in Yueyang, a city with one population of one million.*

***It is the latest in a series of so-called floating cities seen across the globe**, often in China.*

*The emergence of the phenomenon has prompted several theories, including that it **was visible because a portal to another dimension was briefly opened**.*

*Other theories included that it was a **secret government hologram experiment**, known by conspiracy theorists as **Project Bluebeam** - an alleged plot to create a fake second coming to exhort more control over the masses, or even connected to aliens.*

In 1994, research Serge Monast wrote a piece titled *'NASA's Project Blue Beam'*, claiming that NASA and governmental agencies were planning on using holographic and other advanced technologies to bring about a **new world order**.

Science 'Fiction'

Scientific *luminaries* throughout the years have helped push forward the concept that the earth is a ball spinning through space.

The ideas of Greek philosopher Pythagoras, Galileo, 'Sir' Isaac Newton , Johannes Kepler , and Nicolaus Copernicus, among others, contributed to the concept of the 'globe-earth' which is currently taught in schools.

A look at the *'struggles'* of Nicolaus Copernicus demonstrates how the 'globe-earth' *movement* had help from people in high places.

(Copernicus; displaying the 'eye of providence')

It is commonly thought that the 'globe-earth' concept was met with fierce resistance, but that was not the case. In fact, it seems that the opposite was true.

A 2013 article on the Christian Science Monitor (csmonitor.com) titled *'Copernicus and the Church: What the history books don't say'* describes how the idea of a 'globe-earth' was initially accepted with little resistance:

174

Legend has it that Nicolaus Copernicus and the church were at odds over his development of the heliocentric theory, a principle that disputed the widely held belief that Earth was the center of the universe.

Unlike Galileo and other controversial astronomers, however, **Copernicus had a good relationship with the Catholic Church.** It may come as a surprise, considering the Church banned Copernicus' "Des revolutionibus" for more than 200 years. Copernicus was actually respected as a canon and regarded as a renowned astronomer. **Contrary to popular belief, the Church accepted Copernicus' heliocentric theory** before a wave of Protestant opposition led the Church to ban Copernican views in the 17th century.

The Legacy

*"We live on a **hunk of rock and metal that circles** a humdrum star that is one of 400 billion other stars that make up the Milky Way Galaxy which is one of billions of other galaxies which make up a universe which may be one of a very large number, perhaps an infinite number, of other universes. That is a perspective on human life and our culture that is well worth pondering."* – Carl Sagan

To diminish mankind's uniqueness, a narrative was constructed. The narrative is constantly modified and revised to ensure that the official story stands.

The same people responsible for pushing the 'globe-earth' model are also responsible for many of the other accepted 'theories' which are taught in schools.

BANG!

"Create a belief in the theory and the facts will create themselves." –
Joseph Jastrow; 1935

The Big Bang Theory is recognized as a comedic sitcom, while 'science' claims that the theory describes the origin of *reality*.

A 2015 article on universetoday.com titled '*What Is The Evidence For The Big Bang?*' describes the *fascinating* phenomenon:

Almost all astronomers agree *on the theory of the Big Bang, that the entire Universe is spreading apart, with distant galaxies speeding away from us in all directions. Run the clock backwards to 13.8 billion years ago, and everything in the Cosmos started out as a single point in space.* **In an instant,** *everything expanded outward from that location, forming the energy, atoms and eventually the stars and galaxies we see today.* **But to call this concept merely a theory is to misjudge the overwhelming amount of evidence.**

The article goes on to describe the *"evidence,"* which basically consists of observations made by gazing through high-powered telescopes; nothing which can be tested or duplicated in an actual scientific setting.

Such concepts as *"spiral nebulae"* and *"Big Bang Nucleosynthesis"* make it sound as though the concept of a 'Big-Bang' is highly-scientific.

Observation, intuition, and *actual evidence*, on the other hand, demonstrate that matter is not *haphazardly created* from nothing.

Evolve!

*"To suppose that the eye, with all its inimitable contrivances for adjusting the focus to different distances, for admitting different amounts of light, and for the correction of spherical and chromatic aberration, could have been formed by natural selection, seems, I freely confess, **absurd in the highest possible degree.**" –* Charles Darwin; *'On the Origin of Species'*

Charles Darwin is credited with being the originator of the 'theory of evolution,' which essentially **posits that human beings evolved from mammals.**

Darwin came from a wealthy *and powerful* British aristocratic family, and his controversial 'findings' received significant support from those around him.

Besides Aldous Huxley's grandfather, Thomas Henry Huxley (coined "Darwin's Bulldog"), Darwin had other well-placed supporters.

A Canadian Broadcast Corporation (cbc.ca) documentary titled *'Darwin's Brave New World'* outlines the powerful connections, providing readers with a summary of the findings:

*Thomas Huxley, John Hooker, and Alfred Russel Wallace: In one way or another, **these three men are also responsible for the Darwin's theory of evolution.** Each had a pivotal role in supporting Darwin, **pushing him along and providing guidance** as he worked through his theory.*

They shared a love and appreciate of science and of scientific adventure – each man journeyed across the oceans in search of answers. Because of this shared experience, the foursome dubbed their connection the "bond of salt."

179

The theory of evolution receives little resistance. Noted biologist and atheist Richard Dawkins, author of *'The God Delusion'*, describes how evolution and a spherical-earth are no longer up for debate:

*"Evolution is a theory in a special philosophical sense of science, but in terms of ordinary layman's use of language, **it's a fact**. **Evolution is a fact in the same that that it's a fact that the earth is round and not flat; that the earth goes around the sun. Both those are also theories, but they're theories that have never been disproved and never will be disproved.**"*

The Missing Link

(Caricature showing Charles Darwin evolving from an ape)

The missing link - proof of a definitive link between apes and man - **does not exist.**

Oxford Dictionaries defines '*missing link*':

*a thing that **is needed** in order to complete a series, provide continuity, or gain complete knowledge*

The fossil record should have ample proof of the change from ape to man, but instead lone 'discoveries', which often turn out to be hoaxes, are cited as evidence.

'The Piltdown man', which was considered one of the missing links between ape and man, was proven to be a full-blown *and obvious* hoax.

181

(*1915 painting of the Piltdown 'meeting of the minds'*)

A 2012 article on seattletimes.com titled '*Science fiction: when researchers make stuff up*' describes the elaborate hoax, which appears to have been perpetrated by those in 'high-places':

*Tuesday is the centennial of the **grossest fraud of 20th-century science**: Piltdown man. It is a case worth remembering.*

*On Dec. 18, 1912, amateur geologist Charles Dawson **presented to the Geological Society of London** a partial skull. It was purported to be a human ancestor 500,000 to 1 million years old, an age scientists now assign to Homo erectus. Dawson said he had found the fossils in a gravel pit near Piltdown Common, south of London.*

*Dawson had no scientific credentials, but his friend Arthur Smith Woodward did. **Woodward was the keeper of the geological department at the British Museum. He had been at the dig and had seen the jawbone "fly out" of the ground under the blow of Dawson's pick.***

There was a problem with the jawbone. It was from an orangutan only a few hundred years old. It was fitted with two fossilized chimpanzee teeth, filed down to make them look more like human teeth. The cranium fragments were human, from the Middle Ages. All had been treated with an iron solution and acid to make them look older.

Scientists didn't have many fossil skulls in 1912, but none of them looked like a human cranium with an ape jaw.

182

Several scientists, including one from the Smithsonian Institution, argued that the jaw and cranium did not match. **It took 40 years for them to be proved right, and even longer for Dawson to be confirmed as the con man responsible.**

Science is human. It is subject to error and, what's more, malice. *Unlike some other purported paths to truth, science has a way of detecting errors, but not an automatic way. Someone has to do it.*

'The Piltdown Man' is an example of the deception used to perpetrate the 'evolution' lie. The obviously faked remains were showcased as fact, *until the lie could no longer persist.*

Charles Darwin's 'groundbreaking' 1859 book, *'On the Origin of Species'*, is widely considered proof of mankind's 'evolution'.

In the book, Darwin reveals that there are certain *"difficulties"* with the theory:

Some of them are so grave *that to this day I can never reflect on them without being staggered...*

Darwin then goes on to describe some of the *"difficulties,"* exposing how the 'theory' is lacking crucial evidence:

Why, if species have descended from other species by insensibly fine gradations, **do we not everywhere see innumerable transitional forms? Why is not all nature in confusion instead of the species being, as we see them, well defined?**

The fossil record and was not cooperating with 'the theory', so it was eventually modified.

The term *'punctuated equilibrium'* was *devised* to explain what could not otherwise be explained (as defined by dictionary.com):

The theory that new species evolve suddenly over relatively short periods of time (a few hundred to a thousand years), followed by longer periods

183

in which little genetic change occurs. Punctuated equilibrium is a **revision of Darwin's theory that evolution** *takes place at a slow, constant rate over millions of years.*

What Goes Up, Must NOT Come Down

For NASA and other space-related *businesses*, what goes up does not always come down. For everyone else, **what goes up must come down.**

In an *'Ask Us; General Physics: Gravity'* article on nasa.gov, Dr. Eric Christian describes how the earth's spin has *"nothing to do"* with gravity, then describes how the spin *"actually reduces the "gravity" felt by someone at the equator"*:

*Gravity is caused by the **mass of the Earth and has nothing to do with its spinning. The spinning of the Earth actually reduces the "gravity"** felt by someone at the equator as compared to someone at one of the poles.*

Dr. Christian then explains that a phenomenon which cannot be independently proven is *"one of the facts of the Universe"*:

It is just one of the facts of the Universe that everything that weighs anything, pulls other matter towards it, and the more it weighs, the bigger the pull.

185

'Microgravity'

It's not exactly clear when gravity changes once we get into 'space', but Dr. Christian provides a *clear* explanation as to how gravity does not actually turn into zero-gravity, but instead morphs into *"microgravity"* once the 'endless void of space' has been penetrated:

Where is Zero G?

Exactly where does zero gravity start, and can a jet or prop/plane reach zero gravity? At what altitude does oxygen cease to exist?

*Zero gravity is a **bit of a misnomer**. It is used to describe the condition when an object is freely falling with no resistance. You can feel zero G in a plane, roller coaster, or elevator. Gravity is still present, however.* **Something in orbit is essentially freely falling around the Earth.**

*But oxygen and the rest of the atmosphere (mostly nitrogen) just **gradually fade out** and extend hundreds of miles over the surface of the Earth.* **Even where the shuttle and space station are (greater than 400 miles up), there is enough air resistance that there is apparent acceleration of about a millionth of that on the Earth's surface.** *This is why experiments there are called **"microgravity"** experiments, not zero G experiments.*

Logic and reason dictate that matter lighter than air will rise and matter heavier than air will sink, but instead this is attributed to 'gravity'.

Gravity is also used as a method to explain phenomena which otherwise does not occur. For example, water should not be able to rest on an *"oblate-spheroid"* spinning at over 1,000 miles per hour, but gravity explains it away.

When a wet tennis ball is spun rapidly, the water 'gravitates' to the center of the ball and sprays outward. On the spinning-ball earth's surface, the water miraculously 'stays put'.

For reasons beyond what is easily observable, Nikola Tesla explains why the concept of gravity is flawed:

*A good example for such an interaction becomes apparent in gravitation, which should rather be named **universal compression**. I think the material bodies do not gravitate between each other, but it **is the ether** that makes one material body to press to another. **We wrongly call this phenomena gravitation.***

It's All Relative

*"If the facts don't fit the theory, **change the facts**." –* Albert Einstein

The *'Ask Us; General Physics: Gravity'* article continues with Dr. Louis Barbier describing how gravity 'works', making the *clear* connection between *"a sheet of rubber with heavy marbles placed on it"* and the way *"massive objects warp space"*:

Why Does the Universe Have Gravity?

Why does the Universe have gravity? If everything in the Universe was condensed into a singularity before the Big Bang, then gravity must have come from the Big Bang, or gravity predated the Big Bang.

*According to **Einstein's Theory of General Relativity, gravity is the curvature of space that results from a massive object. Think of a sheet of rubber with heavy marbles placed on it. The rubber around the marbles will be curved and smaller marbles placed nearby will roll toward the heavier ones. This is analogous to the way massive objects warp space. This warping is called gravity.***

Tesla describes how the theory of relativity is a garbled mess:

*Einstein's relativity work is a magnificent **mathematical garb which fascinates, dazzles, and makes people blind to the underlying errors.***

188

The theory is like a beggar clothed in purple whom ignorant people take for a king.. its exponents are brilliant men but they are **metaphysicists rather than scientists.**

Tesla further describes how Einstein's theory has no basis in reality:

On a body as large as the sun, it would be impossible to project a disturbance of this kind [e.g., radio to the curvature of space supposed to exist according to the teachings of relativity], but nothing could be further from my mind. **I hold that space cannot be curved, for the simple reason that it can have no properties.** *It might as well be said that God has properties. He has not, but only attributes and these are of our own making.* **Of properties we can only speak when dealing with matter filling the space. To say that in the presence of large bodies space becomes curved, is equivalent to stating that something can act upon nothing. I for one, refuse to subscribe to such a view.**

Join the 'Movement'!

"The best way to control the opposition is to lead it ourselves." –
Vladimir Lenin

In June 2013, US President Barack Obama gave a speech at Georgetown University in which he compared the *ignorance* of 'flat-earthers' with that of 'climate-deniers'.

Articles with the *exact* same title, *'Obama: We Don't Have Time for a Meeting of the Flat Earth Society'*, were **coincidentally** and **simultaneously** run by the BBC, MSNBC, and The Atlantic.

Former U.S. President Barack Obama references the 'flat-earth' in multiple recorded speeches, making one question why such an 'ignorant' concept would be intentionally written into Presidential speeches:

*We're trying to move towards the future, they want to be stuck in the past. We've heard this kind of thinking before. Let me tell you something, if some of these folks were around when Columbus set sail, they must've been **founding members of the Flat Earth Society; they would not have believed that the world was round.***

The former President apparently chooses his words carefully, as "round" and "flat" aren't mutually exclusive concepts. For example, a coin is **round and also flat at the same time**.

In yet another speech, President Obama belittles the flat-earth concept, exposing the fact that people are beginning to become aware of the deception:

*If I say that **the world is round** and someone else says that it's flat,* *that's worth reporting, but you might also want to report on a bunch of the scientific evidence that seems to support the notion that the world is round.*

The mainstream audiences laugh at the President's silly suppositions, **and the Flat Earth Society is there to take the fall.**

For those who have their interest piqued, a trip to the Flat Earth Society's website, tfes.org, is likely their first – **and last** – stop.

The Flat Earth Society's mission statement is straightforward:

*This is the home of the world-famous Flat Earth Society, a **place for free thinkers and the intellectual exchange of ideas**. This website hosts information and serves as **an archive** for Flat Earth Theory. It also offers an **opportunity to discuss** this with the Flat Earth community on our forums.*

While some interesting and pertinent information can be gleaned from the *"intellectual exchange of ideas,"* the content quickly devolves into a muddled mess.

The 'Straw Man'

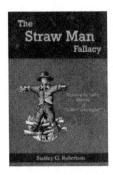

Straw man arguments litter the flat-earth landscape.

Oxford Dictionaries defines *'straw man'* as:

an intentionally misrepresented proposition that is set up because it is **easier to defeat than an opponent's real argument**

With 'debates' surrounding falling off of the edge of the earth, the earth spinning like a Frisbee, and the earth rising to counter 'gravity', those looking into whether the earth is flat are flooded with nonsense and name-calling.

By mixing truth with lies and half-truths, *"truth's protective barriers"* are rarely breached.

"Believe only half of what you see and nothing that you hear." – Edgar Allen Poe

The 'flat-earth' material lies in a sea of garbage, with *disinformation* distorting the legitimate debate.

Merriam-Webster defines *disinformation*:

false information deliberately and often covertly spread (as by the planting of rumors) in order to influence public opinion or obscure the truth

Instead of debating 'the truth', an intellectually ambitious organization would be **seeking and demanding action.**

There are no campaigns or petitions to independently circumnavigate and traverse Antarctica.

There are no initiatives demanding space agencies open themselves up to independent scrutiny, with the risk of losing **ALL** tax dollars.

There are no petitions to investigate companies claiming to use satellite technology, such as cable TV providers, which pass the **exorbitant costs** onto the consumer.

Instead, the public face of flat-earth 'research' manages the debate, with *"fellow believers"* urged to join the 'debate':

*Contact The Flat Earth Society today! We always love hearing from **fellow believers**, those interested in **our views, or the media**!*

Look up

All proof and evidence, other than faked photos and videos, demonstrate that the earth is flat.

Other aspects of our surroundings demonstrate that things we take for granted are different from what we've *been told*.

Improbable coincidences should be the exception, but when it comes to our reality, 'science' instead *tells us* they are the rule.

An article published in 2000 on Astronomy.com, titled '*Why is the Moon exactly the same apparent size from Earth as the Sun? Surely this cannot be just coincidence; the odds against such a perfect match are enormous,'* explains why we should not trust our own eyes:

Believe it or not, it actually is just a coincidence — and a happy one at that. The Moon and Sun have virtually the same angular size in our sky because the Sun is about 400 times wider than the Moon, but it's also about 400 times farther away.

The Sun

The sun, appearing *exactly* the same size as the moon, is said to be **93 million miles** away from earth.

NASA provides a description of the sun, demonstrating humanity's insignificance, in a nasa.gov article titled '*The Sun: The Basics*':

*The sun is a star, a hot ball of glowing gases at the heart of our solar system. Its influence extends far beyond the orbits of distant Neptune and Pluto. Without the sun's intense energy and heat, there would be no life on Earth. And though it is special to us, **there are billions of stars like our sun scattered across the Milky Way galaxy.** If the sun were as tall as a typical front door, the Earth would be the size of a U.S. nickel. The temperature at the sun's core is about 27 million degrees Fahrenheit.*

The article claims that the diameter of the sun is 864,000 miles, which is purportedly 109 times larger than that of the earth.

At 93 million miles away, one would expect the sun's rays to be uniform and straight, but instead the rays spread outwards, hinting that **the sun is likely much closer:**

Said to be over 10,000 degrees Fahrenheit (5,537 degrees Celsius), the source of the sun's heat is a mystery, but NASA claims to have 'cracked the code'.

In a nasa.gov article titled '*Where does the sun's energy come from*', we learn how the immense size and "*a whole lot of gravity*" are *clearly* the cause:

How does a big ball of hydrogen create all that heat? **The short answer is that it is big**. *If it were smaller, it would be just be a sphere of hydrogen, like Jupiter.*

But the sun is much bigger than Jupiter. It would take 433,333 Jupiters to fill it up!

That's a lot of hydrogen. **That means it's held together by a whole lot of gravity**. *And THAT means there is a whole lot of pressure inside of it.*

In fact, the pressure is so intense, and the density so great, that the hydrogen atoms collide with enough force that they literally meld into a new element—helium.

This process—called nuclear fusion—releases energy while creating a chain reaction that allows it to occur over and over and over again.

That energy builds up. It gets as hot as 15 million degrees Fahrenheit in

196

the sun's core. The energy travels outward through a large area called the convective zone. Then it travels onward to the photosphere, where it emits heat, charged particles, and light.

The Moon

(*NASA 'image' and description: "On July 5, 2016, the moon passed between NOAA's DSCOVR satellite and Earth."*)

The moon is purportedly almost 2,000 miles in diameter, and over 200,000 miles away from earth.

We're told the moon, in yet another unprovable miracle, *rotates* in *perfect* synchronicity with earth, never showing us the infamous '*dark side of the moon*'.

From everywhere on earth, the same face of the moon is **always** seen.

Logic would suggest that the moon is not spinning on an axis, but 'science' tells us otherwise. A 2014 space.com article titled '*Does the Moon Rotate?*' provides the *answers*:

*Attentive observers on Earth might notice that the moon essentially keeps the same side facing our planet as it passes through its orbit. This may lead to the question, does the moon rotate? The answer is yes, though it may seem **contrary to what our eyes observe**.*

The reason why our eyes cannot be trusted is clearly explained with "*synchronous rotation*," which also cannot be demonstrated in a laboratory setting, yet commonplace in 'space':

The moon orbits the Earth once every 27.322 days. It also takes approximately 27 days for the moon to rotate once on its axis. As a result, the **moon does not seem to be spinning but appears to observers from Earth to be keeping almost perfectly still.** *Scientists call this* **sychronous rotation.**

The article explains how 'gravity' is the mysterious force keeping the moon in lock-step with earth:

Just like the gravity of the moon affects ocean tides on the Earth, **gravity from Earth affects the moon.** *But because the moon lacks an ocean, Earth pulls on its crust, creating a tidal bulge at the line that points toward Earth.*

Gravity from Earth pulls on the closest tidal bulge, trying to keep it aligned. *This creates tidal friction that slows the moon's rotation. Over time, the rotation was slowed enough that the moon's orbit and rotation matched,* **and the same face became tidally locked, forever pointed toward Earth.**

Nikola Tesla knew that the moon did not revolve on its axis:

The truth is, the so-called "axial rotation" of the moon is a phenomenon **deceptive alike to the eye and mind and devoid of physical meaning. It has nothing in common with real mass revolution characterized by effects positive and unmistakable. Volumes have been written on the subject and many erroneous arguments advanced in support of the notion.** *Thus, it is reasoned, that if the planet did not turn on its axis it would expose the whole surface to terrestrial view; as only one-half is visible, it must revolve. The first statement is true but the logic of the second is defective, for it admits of only one alternative. The conclusion is not justified as the same appearance can also be produced in another way. The moon does rotate, not on its own,* **but about an axis passing thru the center of the earth, the true and only one.**

Nikola Tesla has largely been erased from the annals of history, but his legacy persists. In 1917, Telsa received the "Edison Medal", with noted

199

electrical engineer Bernard Behrend describing Tesla's contribution to society ('*Nikola Tesla Receives Edison Medal*'; Electrical Review & Western Electrician, May 26, 1917):

*Suffice it to say that, were we to seize and to eliminate from our industrial world the results of Mr. Tesla's work, the wheels of **industry would cease to turn, our electric cars and trains would stop, our towns would be dark, our mills would be dead and idle.** Yea, so far reaching is this work, that it has become the warp and woof of industry...*

Perhaps we should take note of Nikola Tesla's *alternative* description of 'the universe':

Earth is a realm; it is not a planet. It is not an object, *therefore,* **it has no edge.** *Earth would be more easily defined* **as a system environment.** *Earth is also a machine, it is a Tesla coil.* **The sun and moon are powered wirelessly with the electromagnetic field (the Aether).** *This field also suspends the celestial spheres with electo-magnetic levitation.* **Electromag levitation disproves gravity because the only force you need to counter is the electromagnetic force, not gravity. The stars are attached to the firmament.**

The Dome

"It may be hard to see tonight, but we are all standing under a glass ceiling." - Hillary Clinton (2016)

(Egyptian 'mythology', with Nut forming 'the dome'; from 'The Gods of the Egyptians Vol. II'; 1904)

The 1888 "Flammarion" engraving below translates to "*a medieval missionary tells that he has found the point where heaven and Earth meet...*":

The earth is surrounded by a powerful radiation field, and whether that field is a physical barrier is open for debate, since **it is illegal to check for ourselves.**

'The dome', referring to the biblical _"firmament,"_ is _coincidentally_ referenced in Antarctica. 'Dome A' is a notable location within the 'frozen tundra' (as described on Antarctica.gov):

With a surface elevation of 4093 m, Dome Argus (Dome A) is the highest place in Antarctica, though one of the least-known places on the globe.

In 2010, the United States Antarctic Program (USAP) reports that '_The Dome is down_':

The dome is down — marking the end of an era and completion of major modernization efforts at the U.S. Antarctic Program's South Pole Station
.

It took a construction crew only a month to unravel the geodesic dome, which for about three decades sheltered polar researchers and support crews who lived at the bottom of the world.

NASA also _coincidentally_ has a fascination with using "domes" in their projects.   .

NASA, on nasa.gov, invites us to '_Go Under the Dome of Silence_' by touring their hi-tech acoustic lab.

The NASA dome in Hawaii, as documented at nasadomehawaii.com, served as home-base for six lucky recruits in an eight-month 'simulation' of life on Mars.

The Mars Dome Project (MDP), as described at nasa.gov, "_is designed to_

grow plants in an enclosed structure under reduced pressure."

NASA partnered with Obscura, at obscuradigital.com, to build a dome theater. A feature on obscuradigital.com titled 'NASA Dome Tour' describes the structure:

*An immersive educational experience, set within a 50-foot **geodesic dome**, was created for a multi-city tour that premiered at the Intrepid Sea, Air and Space Museum in New York City.*

Prominent structures are designed as domes:

The dome – or basilica - in Vatican City was designed by Michelangelo in 1947.

(The Vatican dome from inside)

The Vatican, at vaticanstate.ca, describes how 'the dome' influenced other religious institutions:

*This dome was used as a **model for other domes in the western world**. Among such domes, although built according to different techniques, are those of Saint Paul's in London (1675), Les Invalides in Paris (1680-1691) **and the Capitol building in Washington** (1794-1817).*

'The dome' appears to be featured in a popular logo for one of, if not the, largest entertainment companies in the world:

Movies and shows reference 'the dome':

But of course, **it is all a coincidence**.

Psychotic Society

"Our society is run by insane people for insane objectives ... I think we're being run by maniacs for maniacal ends and I think I'm liable to be put away as insane for expressing that. That's what's insane about it." –
John Lennon

The information in textbooks is lies. The information on television is lies. The entire reality which we inhabit is built on a foundation of lies.

We believe that we are apes who happened to turn human. We believe that our purpose on earth is to make money and pursue superficial endeavors.

But we know better.

The truth is apparent, but most of us refuse to look.

"People don't want to hear the truth because they don't want their illusions destroyed." — Friedrich Nietzsche

Infinite Jest

The 1996 David Foster Wallace novel '*Infinite Jest*' describes a future where humanity has been overstimulated to the point of no return. The title refers to entertainment so engrossing that those who consume it do nothing else, *until they die.*

In his 2005 Kenyon Commencement Address, Wallace describes how our small everyday actions play a much larger role in the grand scheme of things:

*In the day-to day trenches of adult life, **there is actually no such thing as atheism**. There is no such thing as not worshipping. Everybody worships. The only choice we get is what to worship. And the compelling reason for maybe choosing some sort of god or spiritual-type thing to worship -- be it JC or Allah, be it YHWH or the Wiccan Mother Goddess, or the Four Noble Truths, or some inviolable set of ethical principles -- is that pretty much anything else you worship will eat you alive. If you worship money and things, if they are where you tap real meaning in life, then you will never have enough, never feel you have enough. It's the truth. Worship your body and beauty and sexual allure and you will always feel ugly. And when time and age start showing, you will die a million deaths before they finally grieve you. On one level, **we all know this stuff already**. It's been codified as myths, proverbs, clichés, epigrams, parables; the skeleton of every great story. **The whole trick is keeping the truth up front in daily consciousness.**

Worship power, you will end up feeling weak and afraid, and you will need ever more power over others to numb you to your own fear. Worship your intellect, being seen as smart, you will end up feeling stupid, a fraud, always on the verge of being found out. But the insidious thing about these forms of worship is not that they're evil or sinful, it's that they're unconscious. They are default settings. They're the kind of worship you just gradually slip into, day after day, getting more and more selective about what you see and how you measure value without ever being fully aware that that's what you're doing.

And **the so-called real world** *will not discourage you from operating on your default settings, because* **the so-called real world of men and money and power hums merrily along in a pool of fear and anger and frustration and raving and worship of self.** *Our own present culture has harnessed these forces in ways that have yielded extraordinary wealth and comfort and personal freedom; the freedom all to be lords of our tiny skull-sized kingdoms,* **alone at the center of all creation.** *This kind of freedom has much to recommend it. But of course there are all different kinds of freedom, and* **the kind that is most precious you will not hear much talk about** *much in the great outside world of wanting and achieving and [unintelligible --sounds like "displayal"]. The really important kind of freedom involves attention and awareness and discipline, and* **being able truly to care about other people and to sacrifice for them over and over in myriad petty, unsexy ways every day.**

That is real freedom. That is being educated, and understanding how to think. The alternative is unconsciousness, the default setting, the rat race, the constant gnawing sense of having had, and lost, some infinite thing.

Will these times go down in history as *'the dark ages'*, or is there still hope?

Casper Stith

Further Reading?

A book I wrote in 2015 titled *'Satan: Be Afraid, Be Very Afraid'* was composed before I had done any research on the flat-earth. It is clear that Saturn played a key role in past events, and was arguably the 'sun' prior to the deluge.

Satan and Saturn are interchangeable in many respects, and the symbols of Saturn surround us.

Below is a chapter from the book. I encourage others to continue this research, and thank you for *stepping outside the matrix*.

The Original ~~Son~~ Sun God

Is it possible that our entire understanding of the universe is wrong?

Is it possible that the sun shining overhead wasn't always earth's main sun?

According to ancient writings and teachings, a different sun *ruled over* planet earth.

*"It is understood that Velikovsky believed the Earth and Saturn to have o nce moved in close proximity, with the Earth perhaps revolving as a **Satu rnian** moon... The Saturn Myth .. proposes that **Saturn** - fixed at the cele stial pole - loomed massively overhead, a **central sun venerated by all m ankind.** Evidence is presented there for a **Saturnian "polar configuration " as the source of early civilization's dominant symbols."* - David Talbot t and Eve Cochrane, *"The Origin of Velikovsky's Comet"*, Kronos Vol. X N o. 1 (Fall 1984)

Could Satan worship really be *Saturn worship*, layered and disguised thr ough the years?

In grade school we learn that Saturn is the sixth planet from the sun; tha t it's the second largest planet in the solar system (behind Jupiter); that i t's the furthest planet from earth visible with the naked eye; and that it has some pretty cool looking rings surrounding it.

Saturn is made up completely of gas (mostly hydrogen; considered a *'ga s giant'*), and interestingly the hydrogen *"exists in layers that get denser farther into the planet. Eventually, deep inside, the hydrogen **becomes metallic.** At the core **lies a hot interior."***

A planet that far away from the sun shouldn't have a *metallic-hot* core, s hould it?

There are numerous mysteries surrounding Saturn which still defy expla nation, and science.

For example, how could our ancestors have known that Saturn had rings ?

The rings of Saturn are only *supposed* to have been first observed in the seventeenth century, following the invention of the telescope, yet peopl e knew of their existence prior to that time period.

What gives?

Most people never give a second thought to the planet Saturn, yet it ap pears to be the important planet in earth's history.

If Saturn was always simply an irrelevant gas giant barely observable fro m earth, why is the historical record littered with references to Saturn? From mythology to ancient archeology, Saturn **dominates** the landscape .

Have you ever noticed that just about all mythology is based on planets? We simply ignore all of the *myths* and chalk it up to our wild and wacky – and somewhat delusional – ancient ancestors.

All of the ancient '*sun gods*' are attributed to the sun that currently resides at the center of our galaxy, but could that be a mistake?

Could the '*sun*' that many of the ancient cultures revered actually be the planet Saturn?

Well how about that!

The '*sun god*' of the earliest accepted civilization, Mesopotamia (known as the cradle of civilization), was known as *Shamash*.

Shamash was also **the** '*Sun god*' in the Akkadian, Assyrian, Babylonian, and Hebrew pantheons. It is accepted that Shamash was associated with Saturn, not the sun as we know it.

When taking a closer look at the ancient *'sun'* gods, just about all of them are *arguably* representative of the planet/god Saturn.

Velikovsky demonstrates how the gods El, Osiris, Tammuz, and Brahma, among others, represent Saturn. He argues that the sun gods of Egypt, largely attributed to the sun, represent Saturn as well.

Some of the other gods who can arguably be tied back to Saturn are Ba'al, Moloch, Janus, Set, and Adonis – to name just a few more.

There's no denying that the ancient world saw Saturn as *the* all-powerful god. Should we just assume our ancient ancestors were high on peyote and delusional enough to worship an irrelevant planet which could barely be seen?

While most people think that Saturn worship faded out after Roman times, few realize how important Saturn **is** to *modern* culture.

When one takes a hard look at the roots of Christmas, all paths lead to Saturnalia.

Saturnalia, the Roman holiday celebrating Saturn, was *the* most important holiday to the Romans.

The celebration began on December seventeenth and ended December *twenty-fifth*. During Saturnalia, masters often reversed roles with their slaves – to commemorate 'The Golden Age' - a time when *everyone was equal*.

What about Saturn-day? Pardon me, I meant Saturday. Few realize that one of the most, if not the most, anticipated day of the week is named for the *obscure* gas giant Saturn.

Why was this irrelevant gas giant seen as a god? Why was this speck in the sky, barely visible with the naked eye, considered *the* ancient ruler o f the universe?

According to mythology, Saturn ruled the earth during the 'Golden Age.'

The *myths* surrounding the 'Golden Age' point to a time in human history where humanity had *all* of their essential needs met; a time when human indentured servitude had not yet plagued the earth.

Following the mythological 'Golden Age,' the earth was said to have gone through a great trauma, which ushered in a period of *human decline,* **which continues to this day.**

Printed in Great Britain
by Amazon